P9-BUH-398

How Children Learn
# Through Play

BARRON'S

# How Children Learn
# Through Play

Dr. Dorothy Einon

# Contents

First edition for the United States and
Canada published in 2004 by Barron's
Educational Series, Inc.

First published in Great Britain in 2004 by
Hamlyn, a division of Octopus Publishing
Group Ltd, 2–4 Heron Quays,
London E14 4JP

Text © Dorothy Einon 2004

Book design © Octopus Publishing
Group Ltd 2004

The right of Dr. Dorothy Einon to be
identified as the author of this work
has been asserted by her in accordance
with the Copyright, Designs and Patents
Act, 1988.

All rights reserved.
No part of this book may be reproduced in
any form, by Photostat, microfilm,
xerography, or any other means, or
incorporated into any information retrieval
system, electronic or mechanical, without
the written permission of the copyright
owner.

All inquiries should be addressed to:
Barron's Educational Series, Inc.
250 Wireless Boulevard
Hauppauge, New York 11788
http://www.barronseduc.com

Library of Congress Catalog Card No.:
2003116057

International Standard Book No.:
0-7641-2881-7

Printed and bound in China

9 8 7 6 5 4 3 2 1

# Introduction

"To help a child achieve his full potential, parents should ensure that the preschool years are filled with fun"

To the young child, play is learning and so learning is fun. Nature designed children to learn through play because there is simply no other way for them to achieve all that they must achieve in the preschool years. When the child leaves the dimly lit womb, with the regular sounds of his mother's breathing, heartbeat and blood pumping, he enters a world of buzzing and unpredictable stimulation. He is physically helpless, his memory is fleeting, and his ability to communicate, act, or make sense of what is going on around him is almost

By the time he starts school, he can communicate his thoughts and feelings to you in complex language, form hypotheses of why things work the way they do, and recognize and remember familiar places and actions. He can feed and dress himself; play through stories and experiences in his games; run, hop, climb, and jump; draw a man; sing a simple song; deceive you; love you; rebel against your wishes; charm you; melt your heart with a cheeky smile; and sometimes persuade you to do what he wants against your better judgment. It's a *huge* amount to have learned in such a small amount of time.

Unless the child goes willingly and joyfully into learning, there is simply no way he could accomplish so much in the preschool years. We have a name for this learning. We call it play. Play comes naturally to children, and at each stage in their development you will find them playing in the way that is best suited to the tasks that must be learned. Parents naturally want their children to reach their full potential, and this is best achieved by ensuring that the preschool years are filled with fun.

A child's inborn talents develop through experience but children will seek out those experiences only if they find them enjoyable. We cannot learn *for* our children. The easiest way to ensure that they learn is to ensure that their bodies and minds are engaged. No amount of coaching, explaining, correcting, or demonstrating will enrich the child unless this happens.

## Believing in your child

Parents' belief in their child's abilities is vital to his development. Research has shown that children who feel they can do it are more likely to succeed than those who feel they cannot. He may not draw as well as his sister, but while he believes that he can, and you believe he will try, he will almost always do his very best. If you remind him of his sister's superiority he will probably give up drawing altogether, or draw half-heartedly. This does not mean that you must always praise him, however sloppy and inattentive he is to the task in hand. Just let him know you believe in him.

The simple rule is that if you cannot say anything good, it's probably best not to say anything at all. As a general principle, always keep the scales of praise and criticism firmly weighed in the direction of praise. As children grow up they become more self-aware. He knows he is unlikely to be a great football player, but he does not need you to spell it out to him every time he tries to kick a ball. Concentrate instead on letting him know that he is your very own unique and extraordinary boy and that you appreciate his efforts.

## Fostering a creative learning environment

Small children love structure. Give them the choice of a new book and an old familiar one and they will often go for the story they know by heart, especially when they are tired. Play is self-paced and freer than formal learning, but that does not mean it lacks structure or familiar elements. Often play is simply repeating the same task over and over again, but although it may need little thought, it is not pointless. Practice turns the behavior into a skill and

**"**As a general principle, always keep the scales of praise and criticism firmly weighed in the direction of praise**"**

makes it automatic. At other times play is exploring the new—finding out how things work and what needs to be done. Both sorts of play are essential. The first can be carried out almost anywhere; the second needs an environment with as few distractions as possible. The simple rule is that children sometimes need to express themselves freely in their play, sometimes need quite specific training, and always need to practice again what has been learned.

It is not the toys, books, or the physical environment that is most important to the child. It is the child's social environment that really counts. You could fill the house with toys and his waking hours with activity, but if *you* do not engage with him, you add little of value. It is the way caregivers interact with children on a day-to-day and minute-to-minute basis that makes the real difference. Remember that constructive creativity is more about how families interact and how children develop and maintain self-esteem than the expensive toys on the shelf.

### Avoiding distractions

Distractions come from within the child and from outside. Internal distractions arise from

**"** You could fill the house with toys and his waking hours with activity, but if **you** do not engage with him, you add little of value **"**

restlessness, tiredness, hunger, and a tendency to fidget. They are more common in younger children, especially boys. All children need to let off steam at regular intervals, so put on some music and dance or chase them around the yard. It will get the blood pumping back to the brain, and rid them of some of their pent-up energy before you try to settle them down.

External distractions are produced by the environment. They include noise (particularly from the radio or TV), other activities (especially other children playing), and the presence of other toys. If your child is trying to concentrate, it's wise to switch off the TV, light up only the play space rather than the entire room, and put all the toys he is not using out of sight. The fewer distractions he has, the easier it will be for him to concentrate.

## Organizing the day

Because children find chaos difficult and organization reassuring, planning the day's activities can make life easier for all concerned. Remember that it is always best to alternate boisterous activities with calmer ones, and that children enjoy cleaning up quickly to music if you make it into a game. Most children find it easier to concentrate in the morning, and very few small children find it easy to concentrate in the hour before bedtime.

## Parents as teachers

Parents and caregivers know children better than anyone else does. They are able to give the child one-to-one attention, and can choose the right moment to praise and guide the child. This is why they are always a small child's best teacher.

## Points to remember

- Your child has a built-in plan that determines what needs to be learned, and this will push him in the right direction. As he learns to control his hand, he grasps objects. Once he can balance, he will spontaneously hop and jump.
- All children pass through the same stages at about the same age. Watch your child carefully and then look through this book to find an activity that is suitable. If he enjoys what he is doing you will know that you have gotten it right. If he does not, try it again in a few weeks.
- The younger the child, the more likely he is to use actions to ask questions. Most of the time we are happy to encourage him, but some "questions" (actions) are unacceptable or inappropriate. An example of an unacceptable action/question might be "What happens if I pour my drink on the floor?" Distract him. If he persists in "asking" such questions (by pouring all his drinks on the floor, for example), it may be that the question is important to him, so try to find a viable alternative: Let him play at the sink or give him some plastic cups to use in the bath, for example.

# Learning through play most likely occurs when

- Children feel free to express themselves.
- Children grow up in an environment that is open to new experiences and opinions.
- Children are encouraged to manipulate and evaluate ideas.
- Children are allowed to be original.
- Children are encouraged to consider more than one solution to a problem.
- Discipline is firm but not punitive.
- Parents accept some mess.
- Parents do not dismiss what their children achieve.
- Parents have confidence in their children's abilities.
- Parents are sometimes prepared to let children continue playing when they are enjoying themselves.
- Parents provide support and direction without interference.
- Parents demonstrate their own creativity and flexibility.
- Children are exposed to stories.
- Make-believe is encouraged.
- Children have regular contact with other children.

# Whole Body Movement

## By 2–2½ years old

- Can walk and talk, and walk and pull along or carry a toy.
- Can sit on a bike and scoot with his feet.
- Runs with flat feet and short strides but good coordination, but is not able to stop easily or control his speed very well.
- Can briefly stand on tiptoe.
- Holds the rail to climb stairs, leading with the same foot each time, and bringing both feet together on each step.
- Can jump a short distance off the ground and hop briefly on one foot. He makes lots of arm movements but does not crouch.
- Moves his bike (and himself) around an obstacle.

## By 2½ years old

- Can walk along a wall if you hold his hand.
- Can stand on one foot and balance for a few seconds.
- Can go up stairs using alternate feet but still bringing his feet together on each step. He walks down stairs leading with the same foot.
- Can climb ladders and use slides.
- Can jump from the bottom step of the stairs without losing his balance.
- Can copy the movements of an action song.
- Can walk on tiptoe without overbalancing.
- Can use the pedals on his bike—but may still prefer to scoot.
- Can run fast with confidence, but is still flat-footed, and cannot control his direction, speed, or stopping very well.

## By 3 years old

- Can walk across the room on tiptoe.
- Runs more fluidly but is still flat-footed and has difficulty turning or stopping quickly.
- Goes up and down stairs one foot at a time.
- Can jump 5–10 times on both feet and hop 2–5 times on one foot. He crouches to take off but does not bend his knees to land.
- Can jump off a step.
- Can hurdle a jump about 3–4 in. (7.5–10 cm).
- Walks along a wall leading with one foot and drawing the other foot forward to meet it.
- Can walk on a 3 in. (7.5 cm) beam forward 6 ft. (2 m) and backward 3 ft. (1 m).
- May walk along a wall without holding on.

# By 3½ years old

- Starts to go up stairs using alternate feet, but still comes down using a leading foot.
- May be able to genuflect—put a knee on the ground from a standing position.
- Begins to control starts, stops, and turns as he runs.
- Can jump ten times on both feet and hop five times without much spring but with lots of arm movements.
- Can jump down from about 30 in. (80 cm).
- Can walk on a 3 in. (7.5 cm) beam forward 7½ ft. (2.5 m) and backward 4½ ft. (1.5 m).
- Skips with one foot and then walks the second foot to meet it.

# By 4–5 years old

- Goes up stairs using alternate feet, but still comes down using a leading foot.
- Begins to lift off the ground, and also turn, as he runs. By the end of the year he can start and stop at will—but still cannot dodge.
- Tries to gallop but will probably not succeed.
- Hops 7–9 times.
- Can walk on a 3 in. (7.5 cm) beam forward 7½–9 ft. (2.5–3 m) and backward 6 ft. (2 m).
- Can do an 8–10 in. (20–25 cm) standing long jump, a 24–33 in. (60–84 cm) running jump, and a 9 in. (23 cm) hurdle jump.

# By 5–6 years old

- Begins to dodge, running strides increase, and more time is spent off the ground.
- Can gallop, and start and stop at will when running.
- Can hop ten or more times, with more spring in his ankles, knees, and hips.
- Can skip, and by the age of six will skip using the balls of his feet.
- Can jump and reach 2–3 in. (5–7.5 cm).
- Can walk along a 3 in. (7.5 cm) beam 11 ft. (3.3 m) forward and 8 ft. (2.4 m) backward.
- Can climb a rope ladder with the bottom free and may be able to climb a pole or rope. He may try to climb a tree.
- Can do a 15–18 in. (38–45 cm) standing broad jump, a 28–35 in. (70–88 cm) running jump, and a 9 in. (23 cm) hurdle jump.

# Hand–Eye Coordination

## By 2 years old

- Prefers to use either her left or her right hand.
- Uses her thumb in opposition to her forefinger (a pincer grip) or her fingers (a power grip) to pick things up. She can point, prod, stroke, twist, and turn.
- Can thread big beads on a string.
- Can place one block on top of another to build a small tower and put pieces into a puzzle tray.
- May be able to use a simple construction kit.
- Can look at books and point to the pictures.

## By 2½ years old

- Can draw sweeping circles, short lines, and little squiggles.
- Can snip paper but cannot cut around things.
- Can pour, but not accurately, and fill cups at the sink.
- Likes the feel of sand or rice running through her fingers.
- Carries out simple household tasks such as dusting.
- Can dress herself but cannot manage zippers, buttons, or socks very well. She gets her legs in the wrong holes of her pants, her shoes on the wrong feet, and puts her T-shirts on backward.
- Can turn the pages of books.
- Can do a tray puzzle and make a simple construction.
- Likes her hands to be busy, and to fiddle, poke, and investigate.

## By 3 years old

- May be able to copy a simple shape.
- Places things with greater precision and is better at construction skills and jigsaw puzzles. By now she should be able to build brick towers of about eight pieces.
- Can pour accurately and loves water, sand, and dough.
- Feeds herself without too much mess, washes her face and uses a toothbrush, and is getting better at dressing herself.
- Can set the table and sort the laundry. Enjoys helping.
- May be able to draw a crude face.

# By 3½ years old

- Can draw simple figures.
- Can dress herself, although buttons, zippers, and shoes remain a problem.
- Eats and drinks without making a mess.
- Rolls clay into a ball and cuts it with a blunt knife, and may be able to spread soft butter on toast.
- Movements are smoother and more fluid. She lines up jigsaw and construction kit pieces before putting them in. When drawing, she lifts her crayon off the paper and puts it where she wants to start the next line.

# By 4–5 years old

- Draws people with faces, eyes, and noses. They may have legs but probably not bodies. By the end of the year they may have arms. She draws crude houses and possibly cars. She may be able to write her name. She can follow outline drawings and color in, but not accurately or neatly.
- Does jigsaw puzzles with 10–25 pieces, with practice, and is beginning to use small block construction kits. May be able to follow simple instructions on kits—but still needs help.
- Can make more than one successive cut with scissors, but does not cut out accurately.
- Can throw bean bags and small balls, but her aim is poor. She can catch large balls using her arms as well as her hands. Begins to throw overhand.
- Uses a fork to eat and spreads butter on bread.
- Dresses herself in all but the most difficult items.
- Puts soap on her washcloth and toothpaste on her toothbrush. Can dry her hands and face but not her body.

# By 5–6 years old

- Draws trees, animals, people, and houses and begins to assemble them into pictures. Writes her name. Can do simple dot-to-dot drawings, trace a line, copy letters, or draw around shapes. Colors in more neatly but still goes over the lines.
- Uses a knife and fork, but still has problems cutting up meat.
- Uses a hammer, sweeps with a broom, and digs with a trowel. Cuts straight and curved lines with scissors, but cutting out still frustrates her.
- Carries things carefully. She can stand, hold a cup, and talk at the same time.

# Language

## By 2 years old

- Has a vocabulary of around 50 words, and understands several hundred by two. He uses two-word sentences, increasing to three or more words by two and a half.
- Starts to use pronouns (me, she) and prepositions (on, in) but his language is still telegraphic: "Me do it," not "I want to do it"; "Go car" not "Are we going in the car?" Some words and word endings are still missing.
- Expresses recurrence—"more cookie"; absence—"all gone milk"; attribution—"big car"; nomination—"that ball"; agent action—"doggie bite"; and agent action object—"doggie bite bone."

- Understands simple instructions and talks about what he has done. If encouraged, he tells you what he wants.
- Loves having books read to him and remembers simple stories.
- Likes to see your face when you speak to him.
- Knows his full name and perhaps where he lives.

## By 2½ years old

- He learns about 50 new words every month and knows about 1,000 by the age of two and a half. Speaks in 2–3-word sentences, but they are still quite telegraphic.
- Can tell you the names of his family and pets and where he lives.
- Uses the pronouns "I" and "my" frequently but not always correctly. Uses "in" and "on." Says "I walking" and "I doing," adds "s" to words to make them plural—even when he shouldn't ("two sheeps")—and to denote possession ("Jamie's coat"). Can use the past tense ("cup broke") and verb inflections ("doggie bites").
- Can express how he feels, asks what words mean and what objects are called.
- Likes storybooks, and can follow more complex language and stories.

## By 3 years old

- Continues to add about 50 words a month to his vocabulary.
- Uses 2–4-word sentences, often stringing them together to express more complex ideas. He says what he wants and how he feels, and can tell you about his day.
- Can use the negative: "I don't like liver," "This isn't yours," and "I didn't do it."

- Uses the "why" questions constantly—why, what, where. He asks questions using "can," "have," and "did" but the word order is not always correct.
- Says things such as "I am walking," "I do like spaghetti" using auxiliary verbs.

# By 3½ years old

- Knows about 1,250 words, and continues to add about 50 to his vocabulary every month.
- Sentences have a more complex structure: "You think I can do it," "I see what you mean." He can tell a simple story.
- Continues to ask why, what, and where questions but still has difficulty answering them. Uses "if" and "because."

# By 4–5 years old

- Knows 1,800 words and continues to expand his vocabulary by about 50 words a month.
- Speaks in 4–5-word sentences. His language is fluid with fewer errors.
- Understands but probably cannot produce complex sentences such as "He knew that Sam was coming to lunch."
- Uses conjunctions: "I like dessert but I'm too full," "I want to go to the store and buy some cookies."
- Tells his soft toys stories and pretends to read them a book. He talks through his actions as he plays and can often be heard chatting away to himself.

# By 5–6 years old

- Knows more than 2,000 words and will learn about 1,000 a year over the next few years.
- Speaks in longer (6–8-word) sentences.
- Can construct sentences that rely on increasingly complex constructions, such as

"The horse was ridden by the jockey," "I will eat my cereal but I don't want to," "Alfie knew I wanted to draw with that pen," "This is the right way, isn't it?", "That isn't fair, is it?"

# Learning

## By 2 years old

- Investigates why things happen and repeats these investigations over and over again. She watches and becomes engrossed in activities.
- Identifies herself in photographs and in the mirror. She imitates, plays simple pretend games, and talks about objects as if they were human: "Naughty chair," "Moon see me."
- Remembers simple rhymes and songs and joins in actions, and knows if you miss a page in her favorite book.
- Loves outings and new experiences.
- Can divide toys into simple categories, such as puzzles and soft toys, but cannot sort them into smaller groups, such as teddies and bunnies. She can match a red cup with a red saucer.
- Understands that money buys things but has no understanding of its value.

## By 2½ years old

- Gossips, makes up simple stories, remembers yesterday's events and striking happenings from the more distant past. Situations elicit memories—when returning to a place she visited some months ago she will remember where to buy ice cream or that this is where she saw a tree being chopped down. She may not have mentioned the tree since your last visit.
- Repeats things to help herself remember, but is not systematic about this. She can compare the height of two objects and comment on which is bigger but not always accurately.
- Talks as if you share her thoughts and experiences and as if everything centers around her.
- Sorts things on the basis of a single attribute, separating red from blue, for example.
- Believes death is transient. She may think bad things happen because she is naughty, and thinks if A causes B then B also causes A, so if she bumped into the chair, the chair also bumped into her.
- Her understanding of causality depends on how close one thing is to another. For example, she thinks the engine noise makes the car go.

## By 3 years old

- She can easily master a puzzle of 4–6 pieces, and with practice will progress to 10 or more. She will enjoy construction kits, especially those with chunky pieces.
- She remembers where you have left things—and will enjoy looking for your keys. Although she is not systematic, she will remember where she has seen them.
- She will enjoy talking about what you have done. Walking through her experiences will help her learn how to tell a simple story.
- She may be able to find the first letter of her name on road signs.
- She will refer to things she did yesterday.

# By 3½ years old

- Enjoys constructing things but may not plan ahead, so towers topple and things do not fit together as planned. She gets very frustrated when things go wrong.
- Talks as if you share her experiences, describing what she did at playschool as if you were there.

- Assumes you can see what she can see (even though you are facing her).
- Gossips, and explains why she thinks something has happened.

# By 4–5 years old

- Begins to take the perspective of another person and relate it to her own, so she understands that she needs to explain what happened if you were not present.
- Can put together two or more ideas and form a conclusion.
- Plays simple board games but does not use strategy. She remembers where things have been left and does well on games, such as pairs, that involve memory.

- She can count and knows that three is more than two but may not realize that six is more than five. She can coordinate two or more ideas into a single skill.
- Carries out more complex constructions, beginning to plan ahead.
- Tells jokes but does not know why they are funny. Those she makes up lack a punch line.

# By 5–6 years old

- Takes into account what other people see and feel, but still does not use strategies. She may begin to understand jokes.
- Starts to put things in order (from the smallest to the largest) and may be able to match and sort using more than one category—using both shape and color, for example.
- Recognizes letters and one or two words, picking them out on road signs and in books. She can write her name if shown how and may be able to count to ten, but she still does not know that nine is greater than eight.

- Can investigate "what happens if...," watching carefully and offering explanations.
- Remembers what events happened yesterday. She also talks about things in the more distant past.
- Carries out actions more systematically and methodically.
- Logic remains simple; she still thinks there is more orange juice in a tall slim glass than in a short wide one.

# Social Skills

## By 2 years old

- Is affectionate and loving.
- May be shy with strangers and clingy in strange places.
- Has tantrums (one a day is about average) but only with those people he loves. When they are over, he quickly returns to his normal happy self.
- Insists on doing things for himself but is not realistic about his capabilities and gets upset when he fails.
- Loves playing with other children. He joins the games older children lead but may have difficulty playing interactively with children his own age.
- Imitates what parents and caregivers do.
- Shares his toys often but snatches them back unpredictably.
- Knows his gender.

## By 2½ years old

- Is affectionate and loving and will comfort you, or another child, if you are upset.
- May still be clingy but is happy to be left in a familiar place with familiar people (although he may protest when you leave).
- Enjoys playing with other children, and initiates interactions with them without waiting to be included. He is much more able to cope with a crowd. He may form a special friendship with another child, but these friendships are often fleeting. It is now easy to pick out the naturally outgoing children from the naturally shy.
- Insists on doing things for himself but is unrealistic and gets upset when he fails. He has fewer tantrums, and these gradually become more predictable—he will often be testy beforehand and ask to have and do things he knows are off limits.
- Has a distinct sense of self and is protective of his possessions. He shares at playschool but may not do so at home.
- Likes to choose what to eat and wear and is more amenable to family rules.

## By 3 years old

- Is able to play and socialize without checking that you are there. He talks about what he does and is doing, and may even boast.
- Tantrums are less frequent and more predictable, and he is more often sorry and upset afterward and needs to be comforted. He is more amenable to family rules and often helpful and considerate.
- Often finds it hard to share, and is protective about his possessions. He may be mean to his siblings.
- Greets his friends, and chooses his activities because he wants to play with those who are already playing. He plays interactively and can initiate games with other children. He socializes with unfamiliar adults and older children but finds it hard to socialize with unfamiliar children of his own age.
- Imitates what other children and adults do. Sex role stereotypes are deeply ingrained—and will remain so until he is about seven.

# By 3½ years old

- Plays well with other children of all ages, but remains possessive about his toys. He is more likely to play with children of his own sex but does not always do so.

- May have a special friend, and friendships may last longer although they are still often quite fleeting. He is more likely to choose his playmates at playschool than his activities— he joins in with what his friends are doing.

- Plays social pretend games (house, going shopping), learns to boast rather less often as being liked becomes more important to him. He still sometimes plays alone happily in a crowded room.

- Reinforces appropriate sex role behaviors in other children, and girls often talk about boys in a derogatory way—"Boys are naughty and noisy. We don't like to play with them."

# By 4–5 years old

- Plays well with other children, sharing fantasy games, role play, laughter, and conversation. As he approaches five he is able to chat with two or three different people, taking his turn and following the rules of conversation, although he still prefers to talk one to one. He likes to be with friends but is not unhappy when alone. Boys begin to play in slightly bigger groups than girls, and both show a preference for children of their own gender. His view of the opposite sex can be stereotyped, as are his toy preferences, and his peers increasingly influence him.

- Understands that he was, is, and always will be the same gender, but may still believe that if he does "girls" things he might become a girl.

- Begins to understand that other people do not share his thoughts and feelings.

- May have a best friend, and will be unhappy when they disagree.

# By 5–6 years old

- Remains helpful, affectionate, and caring but can also be mean and bossy. He can pick on other children and exclude them from his games. Fights with siblings become more common and will continue to increase over the next 2–3 years. He fights with siblings of the same sex most, and boys fight more than girls— though girls can be manipulative and mean to each other while playing the innocent victim.

- Seems to argue for the sake of it, but is also very protective toward those he fights with.

- Starts to use strategies in games and in life. He manipulates, deceives, cheats, and misleads. He tells lies, avoids taking the blame for things, and may no longer tell you everything he does. The age of innocence is passing, and you are not quite the central pillar of his world as you were a year ago.

- Likes to please but is becoming more competitive, reflecting the values of the society he is raised in. He becomes more moral, understanding right from wrong. He often does the "right thing," even when no one is watching.

- Tells you how he feels, enjoys stories without pictures, and may cry when told a sad story.

# music, song

* Learning to listen
* Musical scales
* Old MacDonald Had a Farm
* Musical circle games
* Songs with actions
* Hit the bottle
* The knee-king rides again
* Clapping games
* I got rhythm
* Listening loiter
* Lotto
* Can I dance on your feet?
* Walk like an Egyptian
* Follow the leader

and dance

# Learning to listen

**CHECKLIST**

| | |
|---|---|
| age 3–4+ | |
| indoor | ✓ |
| no. of children | no limit |
| time | 10 minutes or more |
| help required | ✓ |
| no mess | ✓ |

**EQUIPMENT**

- boxes of rice, split peas, or dried beans, etc.
- saucepan lids, tins, bottles
- metal and wooden spoons
- tape recorder and tapes

## What the child learns

To tune in to the differences between sounds—especially the tone, melody, and rhythmic properties of sounds. To enjoy joining in.

Small children often have trouble concentrating for more than a few minutes, so the first steps in music are mostly about learning to listen and notice the difference between similar sounds and to realize how a certain pattern of sound can express an emotion or build a picture.

## what to do

### WHAT'S THE DIFFERENCE?
Shake a box of rice and a package of split peas. Can the child tell the difference? Now do it behind her back. Can she still tell which is which? You can also try using a wooden spoon and then a metal spoon to hit a saucepan lid.

### COOEE
Practice saying "Cooee" (*coo* is high and *ee* lower). Try shouting it, humming it, whistling it, or whispering it and get her to copy you.

# Making shakers

**SING ALONG**
Small children learn best by doing, so listen to music and sing together.

**SOUND SNAP**
Sing, speak, shout, or play recordings of pairs of different sounds. Some of the sound pairs should be the same; others should be different. If the sounds are the same, the child shouts SNAP.

Play sound snap with recordings of musical instruments, phrases of music, or the duration or pitch of musical notes as children become more skilled.

Small children love to join in music sessions even though they don't know the words. In this way they learn about listening to music, being part of the action, and enjoying it. You can include even the youngest child by making shakers with different fillings for a variety of sounds.

Select tins, plastic bottles, or cartons with lids. Screw-top plastic jars are probably the safest, but tins make the best sound.

Partially fill a container with dried grains, peas, beans, or pasta. Shake to check that the sound is good. Some containers make a hard tinny sound, while others produce more of a slush-slush noise.

For an instant shaker, give her a box of rice, but tape over the top and bottom to avoid spills.

# Musical scales

**CHECKLIST**

| | |
|---|---|
| age 4+ | |
| indoor | ✓ |
| no. of children | no limit |
| time | 10 minutes or more |
| help required | ✓ |
| no mess | ✓ |

**EQUIPMENT**

- something to generate notes: a xylophone, recorder, or your singing voice

## What the child learns

This is a very basic musical skill that all children must learn if they are to sing and play a musical instrument. It's a game to go alongside singing and listening to music, but should not replace them.

Children find it very hard to understand what high and low mean. Because they find it easier to remember actions, it helps to use actions to depict the position of the notes.

## what to do

Select an instrument to make the tones, using 3–4 very different notes. The child stands about four steps from the bottom of the stairs. You sound two notes. If the second one is higher, she goes up a step. If lower, she comes down. If you do not have stairs, she could put her hands on her head for up and on her knees for down.

As the child succeeds you can bring the notes closer together so it is more of a challenge, but try to ensure she usually gets it right.

Encourage an older child to try to "step out" a three-note-sequence. She will manage only after quite a lot of practice.

# Old MacDonald Had a Farm

Here is an action song with noises rather than actions—a great favorite with four-year-olds who love making animal sounds.

**Chorus**

*Old MacDonald had a farm*
*e-i-e-i-o*
*And on this farm he had some [cows]*
   (animal will change)
*e-i-e-i-o*

*With a moo-moo here* (mooing sounds)
*And a moo-moo there* (mooing sounds)
*Here a moo* (sound)
*There a moo* (sound)
*Everywhere a moo-moo* (sounds)

**Chorus**

*Old MacDonald had a farm*
*e-i-e-i-o*
*And on this farm he had some [pigs]*
   (animal will change)
*e-i-e-i-o*

*With an oink-oink here* (oink sounds)
*And an oink-oink there* (oink sounds)
*Here an oink* (sound)
*There an oink* (sound)
*Everywhere an oink-oink* (sounds)

At this point, older children can continue by repeating the first animal verse. Younger children will find it easier to do one animal at a time. Repeat the chorus in order to add a new animal.

Continue adding animals, along with their sounds (horse/neigh, sheep/baa, etc.) until the children can't think of any more.

| CHECKLIST | |
| --- | --- |
| age 4+ | |
| indoor/outdoor | ✓ |
| no. of children | no limit |
| time | 10 minutes |
| help required | ✓ |
| no mess | ✓ |

**EQUIPMENT**
none required

## What the child learns

To join in with the sounds even before she knows the words. Repeated sounds are marvelous for picking up the rhythm of songs, which in turn is great practice for later reading skills.

# Musical circle games

| CHECKLIST | |
|---|---|
| age 2–6 | |
| indoor/outdoor | ✓ |
| no. of children | at least 3 |
| time | 10 minutes or more |
| help required | ✓ |
| no mess | ✓ |

**EQUIPMENT**
- cloth bag or sock
- source of music (optional)

## What the child learns

The rhyming songs used in these games encourage children to look out for the little sounds that make up words and notes—a vital skill for reading and appreciating music.

Musical circle games have an ancient history. Many of them started life as formal dances; others were dances to encourage the fertility of the land or the return of the summer sun. Similar games are played everywhere in the world.

## what to do

### Here We Go 'Round the Mulberry Bush

Children form a circle, holding hands, and begin by singing the chorus.

**Chorus**
*Here we go 'round the mulberry bush,
the mulberry bush, the mulberry bush.
Here we go 'round the mulberry bush,
So early in the morning.*

Children then stop and sing a stationary verse with accompanying actions. The chorus is sung between each verse. Let each child decide on the actions of one verse.

*This is the way we brush our teeth, brush our
   teeth, etc.
This is the way we comb our hair, comb our
   hair, etc.*

### Ring around the Rosey

Children dance around and fall down as the words suggest. They then jump up and dance around again. Simple and satisfying, even for the youngest children.

*Ring around the rosey,
A pocket full of posies,
Ashes, ashes,
We all fall down.*

## Skip to My Lou

This is also a circle game but played in a rather different way. For this game, children sit in a circle and one child is chosen to carry the bag (you could use a sock). She skips slowly around the outside of the circle while the children sing. You can sing any song you like, just play music or sing this:

*Skip, skip, skip to my Lou*
*Skip, skip, skip to my Lou*
*Skip, skip, skip to my Lou*
*Skip to my Lou, my darling*

When the music or singing stops, the child must skip once around the circle and drop the bag behind one of the seated children, all of whom should be looking straight ahead. The child with the bag must jump up and race the skipper around the circle back to the empty spot. The child who reaches it first sits down and the loser skips in the next round.

# Songs with actions

| | |
|---|---|
| indoor/outdoor | ✓ |
| no. of children | no limit |
| time | 10 minutes or more |
| help required | ✓ |
| no mess | ✓ |

**EQUIPMENT**
none required

## What the child learns

He learns to remember a sequence of actions associated with specific words and a tune. In making the movements in time to the song, he learns to listen to the rhythm. Getting all the actions right gives young children a sense of achievement and a feeling of confidence.

Small children find it much easier to join in a song if it has actions—even if they forget the words they remember what to do. They also learn how much fun it is to join in.

## what to do

**I'm a Little Teapot**

*I'm a little teapot short and stout*
ACTION: ONE HAND ON HIP

*Here is my handle, here is my spout*
ACTION: ONE ARM MAKES A SPOUT

*When I get all steamed up, hear me shout*
*Tip me over and pour me out.*
ACTION: BEND FROM THE WAIST IN A POURING MOVEMENT

**Miss Mary Mack**

*Miss Mary Mack, Mack, Mack*
ACTION: TOUCH KNEES THREE TIMES

*All dressed in black, black, black*
ACTION: TOUCH SHOULDERS THREE TIMES

*With silver buttons, buttons, buttons*
ACTION: CLAP HANDS TOGETHER

*All down her back, back, back.*
ACTION: CLAP PARTNER'S HANDS THEN SPIN AROUND

Repeat the actions for the following two verses:
*She sent her mother, mother, mother*
*For fifty cents, cents, cents*
*To see the elephant, elephant, elephant*
*Jump over the fence, fence, fence.*

*He jumped so high, high, high*
*He reached the sky, sky, sky*
*And never came back, back, back*
*'Til the first of July, ly, ly.*

## Miss Polly Had a Dolly

*Miss Polly had a dolly who was sick, sick, sick*

**ACTION:** FOLD ARMS AND ROCK THE BABY

*So she called for the doctor to come quick, quick, quick*

**ACTION:** TELEPHONING

*The doctor came with his bag and his hat*

**ACTION:** PAT TOP OF HEAD

*And he knocked on the door with a rat-a-tat-tat*

**ACTION:** KNOCKING ON DOOR

*He looked at the dolly and he shook his head*

**ACTION:** SHAKE HEAD

*He said "Miss Polly, put her straight to bed"*

**ACTION:** WAG FINGER

*He wrote on a paper for a pill, pill, pill*

**ACTION:** WRITING

*"I'll be back in the morning with my bill, bill, bill"*

**ACTION:** PUT HAND OUT FOR MONEY

# Hit the bottle

CHECKLIST

| | |
|---|---|
| age 4+ | |
| indoor | ✓ |
| no. of children | no limit |
| time | 30 minutes–1 hour |
| help required | ✓ |
| no mess | unless a bottle tips over |

EQUIPMENT

- 8 sturdy glass bottles
- water
- wooden spoon or chopstick

## What the child learns

How to work things out and do things for herself, how to listen, and how to put things in a sequence from low to high. She also becomes directly involved in music.

**This is a simple activity that gives the child experience in making different sounds. If you have a good ear you may be able to tune the bottles to the musical scale.**

## what to do

Take eight glass bottles or jars and fill them with water to different levels.

If you can, tune them against a musical instrument. If not, just do your best to make them all sound different!

Let the child tap each bottle with a wooden spoon and encourage her to make her own music.

For a younger child, simply fill a few assorted jam jars and bottles with different amounts of liquid and let her tap the jars with a chopstick.

# The knee-king rides again

Riding on an adult knee is a firm favorite with all toddlers. Since we play these games with small children from babyhood, these are often the songs and rhythms they know best. Most rhymes contain two different elements: a ride—sometimes at varying speeds—and an inevitable fall.

## what to do

### To Market, To Market

ACTION: SIT THE CHILD ON YOUR KNEE AND JOG ALONG AT A STEADY PACE AS YOU CHANT

*To market, to market, to buy a fat pig*
*Home again, home again, jiggety-jig*
*To market, to market, to buy a fat hog*
*Home again, home again, jiggety-jog*
*To market, to market, to buy a plum bun*
*Home again, home again, market is done.*

### Father and Mother

ACTION: IF YOU WISH, ADD A FALL WHEN THE KNEES COLLAPSE

*Father and mother and Uncle John*
*Went to market one by one*
*Father fell off*
*Mother fell off*
*But Uncle John went on and on and on and on.*

### This Is the Way the Gentlemen Ride

ACTION: IF YOU WISH, INCLUDE A CHANGE OF PACE—A SMOOTH, GENTLE BUMP FOR THE GENTLEMEN; A LOPING, SIDE-TO-SIDE MOTION FOR THE FARMER; QUICK, SMALL BUMPS FOR THE LITTLE ONES

*This is the way the gentlemen ride*
*Bumpety, bumpety, bump*
*This is the way the farmers ride*
*Gallumpety, gallumpety, glump*
*This is the way the little ones ride*
*Bumpety, bumpety, bump*

**CHECKLIST**

| | |
|---|---|
| age 2 | |
| indoor | ✓ |
| no. of children | 1 |
| time | 10 minutes or more |
| help required | ✓ |
| no mess | ✓ |

**EQUIPMENT**
none required

## What the child learns

This is one of the best ways of emphasizing the rhyme of a song to the child. It also helps the child to hear the little sounds that make up words, which is good for the development of sounding-out skills needed for reading and spelling.

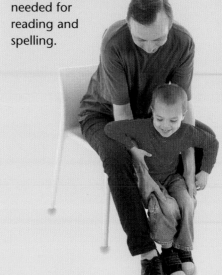

# Clapping games

**CHECKLIST**

| | |
|---|---|
| age 2–6 | |
| indoor/outdoor | ✓ |
| no. of children | pairs, or a child and an adult |
| time | 10 minutes or more |
| help required | for younger children |
| no mess | ✓ |

**EQUIPMENT**

none required

## What the child learns

Clapping games are good for establishing a rhythm, for anticipation, and for improving manual dexterity.

Clapping emphasizes the rhythm of a song. From the simplest game of Pat-a-Cake to more elaborate clapping rhythms, there is something here to suit all ages and skills.

## what to do

### Pat-a-Cake

A two-year-old will readily clap along to Pat-a-Cake.
*Pat-a-cake, pat-a-cake, baker's man*
*Bake me a cake as fast as you can*
*Prick it and pat it and mark it with B*
*And put it in the oven for Baby and me.*

### Under the Apple Tree

By three she can manage a simple rhythm of a single clap followed by a two-handed slap of her partner's hands as they sing.
*As I sat under the apple tree*
*A birdie sent his love to me*
*And as I wiped it from my eye*
*I said thank goodness cows can't fly.*

### If You're Happy and You Know It

This is a favorite with children of all ages.
*If you're happy and you know it clap your hands*
ACTION: CLAP HANDS TWICE
*If you're happy and you know it clap your hands*
ACTION: CLAP HANDS TWICE
*If you're happy and you know it and you really want to show it*
*If you're happy and you know it clap your hands.*
ACTION: CLAP HANDS TWICE

For subsequent verses, change the action to keep the children interested. Here are a few examples, but the possibilities are endless!

*If you're happy and you know it stamp your feet, etc.*
*If you're happy and you know it nod your head, etc.*
*If you're happy and you know it shout hooray, etc.*

## Bingo

By five, children can understand the concept of replacing words (or letters, in this case) with claps. *Bingo* is a favorite. After singing the song once through, the child repeats the song but claps on the letter B instead of saying it. The claps are repeated for each letter each time the verse is sung, until the child is clapping the word to the rhythm of the song.

*There was a farmer had a dog*
*and Bingo was his name-o*
*B-I-N-G-O*
*B-I-N-G-O*
*B-I-N-G-O*
*and Bingo was his name-o.*

ACTION:
*There was a farmer had a dog*
*and Bingo was his name-o*
CLAP-I-N-G-O
CLAP-I-N-G-O
CLAP-I-N-G-O
*and Bingo was his name-o.*

*There was a farmer had a dog*
*and Bingo was his name-o*
CLAP–CLAP-N-G-O
CLAP–CLAP-N-G-O
CLAP–CLAP-N-G-O
*and Bingo was his name-o.*

REPEAT UNTIL ALL LETTERS ARE CLAPPED OUT.

# I got rhythm

CHECKLIST

age 2–6

| | |
|---|---|
| indoor/outdoor | ✓ |
| no. of children | no limit |
| time | 10 minutes–1 hour |
| help required | ✓ |
| no mess | ✓ |

**EQUIPMENT**

- drums or drum substitutes such as cookie tins or saucepans
- drumsticks or substitutes such as chopsticks

## What the child learns

To recognize rhythm when he hears it and to see music in many of the sounds in the world around him. To pick out the rhythm and beat of both conventional music and other everyday sounds. A greater understanding of what music is all about when he sees what it is that music often describes.

The world is full of rhythms—the ticking of a clock, the sound of car wheels, the click and hum of machinery. Make sure the child is aware of these rhythms, and buy or make him a drum so that he can practice making a rhythm himself.

## what to do

### GAINING AWARENESS

Teach the child to listen for rhythms. Stop and listen to the traffic noises. Listen to the waves on the beach, the clatter of the subway train, the chirping of the birds, the swishing and twirling of the washing machine.

Emphasize a rhythm you are listening to together: clap it out, stamp it, or say it together: *b-b-b-bm b-b-b-bump* for car wheels going over a speed bump or say the following rhyme while chopping vegetables:

*Chop, chop, choppity chop,*
*Cut off the bottom,*
*Cut off the top.*
*Whatever is left,*
*Put in the pot.*

Put his hand on the washing machine. Can he feel the rhythm of the vibration when the washer gets to the spin cycle?

When the child is sitting on your lap, tap his back in time to the music or jiggle him on your knee as you tap your foot.

## PUTTING IT INTO PRACTICE
Buy a toy drum. If you can find one, a small African drum has a good tone.

Encourage him to use his hands to pat, punch, hit, and stroke the drum. Let him try hitting the drum with padded and unpadded sticks, and using a stiff brush to stroke it.

Improvise a temporary drum from a cookie tin, a saucepan, or a baking pan and compare the sounds they make.

If you feel you cannot cope with a drum, consider a tambourine instead. He can hit it and shake it, but it never gets as noisy.

Find some music with a good strong regular beat (1960s rock and roll is good) and let the child play along.

# Popstars

Pop songs often have heavily emphasized rhythms and very few notes, so they are ideal for small children to sing and dance along to. This teaches them to move to the music and how to express the rhythm of a song in their movements.

Encourage the child to completely play the part by dressing up in a suitable outfit and using a microphone (a wooden spoon would do).

Put on the music and let the child sing and dance. For a child who really enjoys the game, look for a karaoke kit.

# Listening loiter

**CHECKLIST**

age 3–4+

| | |
|---|---|
| outdoor | ✓ |
| no. of children | no limit |
| time | 30 minutes or more |
| help required | ✓ |
| no mess | ✓ |

**EQUIPMENT**

none required

## What the child learns

To be observant and to pay attention to detail, to be calm and thoughtful, to talk about her experience and to feel close to those who share it.

In the city, we are so used to ignoring the sounds around us that we rarely pay attention to anything in the background. Listening Loiter is a nice, quiet, and calming activity for a day when your child is upset or out of sorts.

## what to do

Take a walk down the street and into the park. Listen to the sounds of the traffic and to other sounds that are not related to traffic: bird song, a plane flying high, the swish of the fallen leaves underfoot, the sound of the wind in the trees, and music coming from a house, for example.

When you arrive at the park, listen to the different sounds of the park: children playing, ducks quacking, a mower cutting the grass.

Then concentrate on the distant sounds of the street. Can you find a spot in the park where the street sounds are quietest? Can you find a spot where you cannot hear them at all? Remember that a hill or building will block out the sound.

Encourage the child to make some new street and park sounds: jump on the drain cover, pull a stick along the railings, shake a branch on a tree, or throw a stone in the pond, for example.

# Lotto

This is a game for slightly older children that encourages careful listening. You could play it with a group of children, or a child could play by himself, turning the tape recorder on and off between the different sounds.

## what to do

Assemble pictures of things that make noises, such as animals, machinery, cars, or musical instruments. Using a tape recorder, record the noise that the object in each picture makes.

Give each child six different pictures on cards. Starting at a random point on the tape, play the noises back to the children.

When a child recognizes that something on one of his cards made the noise, he turns the card over.

The first child to turn over all his cards is the winner.

To play with one child, just put out six or more cards and let him control the tape.

Start by using everyday sounds, then try a group of musical instruments: a drum, cymbals, a piano, a violin, a trumpet, and a flute, perhaps.

**CHECKLIST**

| | |
|---|---|
| age 3–4+ | |
| indoor | ✓ |
| no. of children | 1–4 |
| time | 20 minutes or more |
| help required | ✓ |
| no mess | ✓ |

**EQUIPMENT**
- **picture cards**
- **tape recorder**

## What the child learns

To recognize sounds. To listen to the tone, melody, and rhythmic properties of sounds.

# Can I dance on your feet?

## CHECKLIST

| | |
|---|---|
| age 3–4+ | |
| indoor | ✓ |
| no. of children | 1 at a time per adult |
| time | 10 minutes or more |
| help required | ✓ |
| no mess | ✓ |

## EQUIPMENT

• source of music

## What the child learns

To think very carefully about the way that she moves, to take small cues about someone else's movement. As she improves, to move in time with another person's movements.

This is an activity I did with my grandfather—and I still remember it! It produces laughter and high spirits, yet it also teaches the child to follow and fit in with the movements of others, an essential skill for a dancer.

## what to do

Put on a fairly slow tune.

The child takes off her shoes and puts one foot on top of each of your feet and you hold her in place.

In theory, then you dance. In practice, it will probably take some time to learn how to move together. Start by walking up and down in one direction first, then try taking steps to the side.

If it gets too difficult, you can always pick her up and dance with her in your arms.

# Walk like an Egyptian

**CHECKLIST**

| | |
|---|---|
| age 3–4+ | |
| indoor | ✓ |
| no. of children | no limit |
| time | 10 minutes or more |
| help required | ✓ |
| no mess | ✓ |

**EQUIPMENT**
• source of music

## What the child learns
To be aware of his body and the way other people interpret his movements. To plan what to do and carry out that plan. Thinking about how to interpret the movement of another creature is the first, easy step toward interpreting a musical sound in movement.

In order to dance, it is necessary to be aware of our bodies as well as be able to express the rhythm and mood of the music. This simple, fun activity encourages children to be aware of how they are moving.

## what to do
Encourage the child to walk and move to music in different ways—for example, hop like a frog, creep like a cat, slither like a snake, and, yes, walk like an Egyptian if he knows how!

Anything goes, so get him to move around to the music in many silly or exaggerated ways.

# Follow the leader

| | |
|---|---|
| indoor/outdoor | ✓ |
| no. of children | no limit |
| time | 10 minutes or more |
| help required | ✓ |
| no mess | ✓ |

**EQUIPMENT**

• pen and paper for writing down rhythm

## What the child learns

This game teaches a child to follow an action. The easiest way for her to learn is to "do," and the easiest way to do it is with an action.

In making music, listening skills come first, then comes recognition, and finally, repetition. Once a child knows how to listen, she is ready to start playing with her first musical instrument: her body. There are many different rhythms she can use and many patterns she can copy.

## what to do

Show her how she can start a rhythm using her body. She can clap with her hands, stamp with her feet, tap fingers on the palm of her hand, bang her shoes together, slap her thighs, slap her blown-up cheeks, and click her tongue with her mouth open or closed.

Begin by using just one of these sounds to make a rhythm for her to copy. Make it simple at first, a regular rhythm in a short sequence gradually mixing short and long spaces.

Once she can copy a rhythm using one part of her body, she can start to make mixed rhythms: two stamps and a clap, two claps and a slap to her thigh, and so on.

Introduce her to songs she can clap out. Use those she knows well.

By four years old she will be able to "read" a rhythm you have written down for her. Use a long line for a long sound and a short one for a brief note.

## The Eensy Weensy Spider

You could play this as an action song in the car or sitting on the sofa together.

*The eensy weensy spider climbed up the water spout*

**ACTION:** PUT TIP OF LEFT THUMB ON RIGHT FOREFINGER AND RIGHT THUMB ON LEFT FOREFINGER. OPEN THE BOTTOM PAIR, TWIST THEM OVER THE TOP PAIR AND REJOIN THE LOWER PAIR ABOVE. REPEAT SO YOU CLIMB HIGHER AND HIGHER ON YOUR LEGS

*Down came the rain and washed the spider out*

**ACTION:** HOLD HANDS UP AND WIGGLE FINGERS DOWN TO INDICATE RAIN

*Out came the sun and dried up all the rain*

**ACTION:** MAKE A BIG SWIRL WITH ONE OR BOTH ARMS

*And the eensy weensy spider climbed up the spout again.*

**ACTION:** CLIMB AGAIN

# Words and

- Counting rhymes
- Washday sorting
- What it says on the box
- ABC rhymes
- Making a list
- License plates
- Out and about
- Counting out and about
- Learning scrapbook
- Teddy's tea party
- Just measuring
- Weighing rice
- Baby clinic
- Name that window
- In the bag
- Let's cook together
- What's for snack?
- Tongue twisters
- A deck of cards

numbers

# Counting rhymes

| | |
|---|---|
| age 3–4+ | |
| indoor | ✓ |
| no. of children | no limit |
| time | 10 minutes or more |
| help required | ✓ |
| no mess | ✓ |

**EQUIPMENT**
none required

## What the child learns

To count, and to begin to understand what the numbers mean; for example, two is one plus another one, one less than ten is nine, and so on. When the sequence is in doubt, to say the rhyme. Rhyming is also an essential skill for reading and spelling, encouraging the child to notice the similarities between the little sounds that make up words.

Learning to count is the first step in understanding what numbers mean. When children first count, it is just a rhyme like other rhymes; they probably understand 1-2-3 but cannot visualize what 6-7-8 mean. Once the child knows the sequence 1-2-3-4-5-6-7-8-9-10, she can begin to understand what the numbers mean; adding, subtracting, and pointing as you count reinforce this. Small children often get the numbers out of sequence, so they need plenty of practice.

## what to do

Say the rhymes to the children in quiet moments and encourage them to join in by counting out the numbers on their fingers and toes and, if there are any, doing any actions suggested by the rhyme.

### One Two, Buckle My Shoe

*One, two, buckle my shoe;*
*Three, four, knock at the door;*
*Five, six, pick up sticks;*
*Seven, eight, lay them straight;*
*Nine, ten, a big fat hen;*
*Eleven, twelve, dig and delve;*
*Thirteen, fourteen, maids a-courting;*
*Fifteen, sixteen, maids a-kissing;*
*Seventeen, eighteen, maids are waiting;*
*Nineteen, twenty, my plate's empty.*

### Fish Alive

*One, two, three, four, five*
*Once I caught a fish alive*
*Six, seven, eight, nine, ten*
*Then I let it go again*
*Why did you let it go?*
*Because it bit my finger so*
*Which finger did it bite?*
*This little finger on the right.*

The following rhyme practices simple subtraction:

## Ten Green Bottles

*Ten green bottles standing on
    the wall,*
*Ten green bottles standing on
    the wall,*
*And if one green bottle should
    accidentally fall*
*There'll be nine green bottles
    standing on the wall,*
*Nine green bottles standing on
    the wall,*
*Nine green bottles standing on
    the wall,*
*And if one green bottle should
    accidentally fall*
*There'll be eight green bottles
    standing on the wall*

Continue until there are no
bottles left.

Here is a simple rhyme that
counts people:

## This Old Man

*This old man, he played one*
*He played knick-knack*
*On my thumb*
ACTION: HOLD UP FIRST FINGER FOR
"ONE," AND THEN TAP ONE THUMB ON
TOP OF THE OTHER.

### Chorus

*With a knick-knack, paddy whack,*
*Give a dog a bone,*
*This old man came rolling home.*
ACTION: PUT ONE FIST ON TOP OF THE
OTHER FOR "KNICK-KNACK, PADDY
WHACK," PRETEND TO HAND THE BONE
TO THE DOG, AND THEN ROLL ONE ARM
OVER THE OTHER.

# Washday sorting

**CHECKLIST**

| | |
|---|---|
| age 3–4+ | |
| indoor | ✓ |
| no. of children | no limit |
| time | 10 minutes or more |
| help required | to start |
| no mess | ✓ |

**EQUIPMENT**
- basket of dirty laundry
- basket of clean laundry

## What the child learns

To sort into groups, to understand things can sometimes be sorted more than one way, and to join in the family chores as a matter of course.

To understand what numbers mean, children have to understand what counting is really about, which is surprisingly difficult. It's easy to point to a tree and say the word, but how do you point to "three?" To know what is meant by "three," children have to notice what three cats and three teapots have in common. The first step is to learn how to separate things into different groups.

## what to do

Sort the dirty laundry into whites and colors.

Sort the dirty laundry into wool, cotton, and man-made fabrics. This will be hard for a three-year-old, but a four-year-old should manage to follow your example.

Sort the clean laundry into clothes and other things.

Sort the clean laundry into Mom's, Dad's, and mine.

# What it says on the box

This is another sorting game. Children find objects to put into two or more bags or boxes. She can sort by color, size, shape, or ownership. What goes in each? Well, it "says" on the box.

## what to do

Give her a large box and a small box for her to sort items by size, and give her two bags with red or green tags for her to sort by color.

Start her off with building blocks of different sizes and colors. Next, ask her to collect things from around the house to put into each box and bag. You will possibly need to supervise this one and set some ground rules: for example, avoid breakables and rummaging in closets.

In the yard, get her to sort flowers by color, but do not let her pick them unless there are plenty.

In the car, give her a bus bag and a truck bag. She should put buttons or pennies into the right bag each time she sees a bus or a truck.

Get her to count how many objects are in each bag or box.

**CHECKLIST**

| | |
|---|---|
| age 3–4+ | |
| indoor/outdoor | ✓ |
| no. of children | no limit |
| time | 10 minutes or more |
| help required | ✓ |
| no mess | ✓ |

**EQUIPMENT**
- two or more bags, boxes, pails, or cartons
- objects to collect from around the house, yard, or toy chest
- buttons and pennies for use in the car

## What the child learns
To sort into groups, to understand that things can sometimes be sorted more than one way, to count.

# ABC rhymes

| | |
|---|---|
| indoor | ✓ |
| no. of children | no limit |
| time | 10 minutes or more |
| help required | ✓ |
| no mess | ✓ |

**EQUIPMENT**

none required

## What the child learns

These rhymes help children learn the names of the letters (different from the sounds of the letters), which is essential in being able to ask for help when writing and spelling. A great deal of practice is needed.

Learning the alphabet is a lot harder than learning to count to ten because there are more letters and more opportunities to make mistakes. The child needs a lot of practice.

## what to do

The easiest rhyme is the sing-song version of the alphabet.

*A B C D E F G*
*H I J K L M N O P*
*Q R S, T U V*
*W X, Y, and Z*
Now I know my ABCs,
*A B C D E F G*

Here is a more complicated rhyme:

| | | | |
|---|---|---|---|
| A | *was an apple pie,* | E | *eats it* |
| B | *bit it* | F | *fought for it* |
| C | *cut it* | G | *got it* |
| D | *dealt it* | H | *had it* |
| | | I | *inspected it* |
| | | J | *jumped it* |
| | | K | *kept it* |
| | | L | *longed for it* |
| | | M | *mourned for it* |
| | | N | *nodded at it* |
| | | O | *opened it* |
| | | P | *prepared for it* |
| | | Q | *questioned it* |
| | | R | *ran for it* |
| | | S | *stole it* |
| | | T | *took it* |
| | | U | *upset it* |
| | | V | *viewed it* |
| | | W | *wanted it* |

**XYZ and ampersand**
*All wished for a piece in hand.*

# Making a list

Children make their first attempts to write at about the same time that they start to draw. Look for the little lines of scribble rather than the big sweeps. If you encourage these by calling them "your writing," he will sometimes sit and write rather than draw.

## what to do

When you make a shopping list, give your child a pen and a piece of lined paper so he can make his own list. He does not need to do "real writing" any more than his first drawings need to be recognizably "real" objects. If you encourage him to make lines of scribble, he will gradually change these into lines of writing.

Look at his scribbles and pick out any letters he has made by chance: "Look, you wrote a real *n*." He will be proud of this, and next time he may look for that *n* by himself. Then he may start to make them intentionally.

With encouragement, he will gradually begin to write. Just let him continue at his own pace. Praise the letters he produces but do not down-play his scribbles. If he thinks his writing is appreciated, he is much more likely to continue than if he feels he can no longer do it.

**CHECKLIST**

| | |
|---|---|
| age 3–4+ | |
| indoor | ✓ |
| no. of children | no limit |
| time | 10–30 minutes |
| help required | ✓ |
| no mess | ✓ |

**EQUIPMENT**
- paper
- pencil

## What the child learns

That writing is a useful skill and one that he can master. To recognize letters and, in time, produce them to order.

# License plates

**CHECKLIST**

| | |
|---|---|
| age 3–6+ | |
| outdoor | ✓ |
| no. of children | no limit |
| time | as long as it takes to get where you are going |
| help required | ✓ |
| no mess | ✓ |

**EQUIPMENT**

• parked cars

## What the child learns

To recognize letters, words, and numbers; to be observant; and to realize the many contexts in which letters and numbers are found. To do simple mental arithmetic.

This is a simple game to play when you are out and about. It can be played in various ways, depending on the age and knowledge of the child. At its simplest you look for letters or numbers on license plates. At its most complex, you take the letters in turn and even spell out words. A word of warning: There will be less squabbling about what might have been seen if you restrict the game to parked cars.

## what to do

As you walk down the street look at the license plates on cars and find different letters and numbers. For the youngest child, start with the letters he knows or those that are easiest to spot, like S (for snake) and L (for leg with a foot on the bottom).

Look for the numbers 1 to 10. Give each child a bag to put his (prepared) initial or age into and see how many he can find.

Show younger children how to use their fingers to count and give them a number under ten to find. They can then count this number on their fingers.

Get older children to add up the numbers on certain license plates. Can they find a license plate that adds up to ten?

Encourage older children to spot words on the license plates, or make new ones by reordering the letters.

# Out and about

Doing the shopping may take longer when you make it into a game that involves the children, but it is a lot less stressful when you do not need to deal with the tantrums, fractiousness, and bad behavior that boredom provokes.

## what to do

On the way to the stores, look for the child's initials on road names, store names, and advertisements. Look for her age on door numbers, bus numbers, and license plates.

In the supermarket, get her to find the foods she likes best and to look for her initials on cans and packages.

Play a round of *I Spy* in each aisle of the supermarket.

Count how many checkouts are open, and how many people are in line there.

**CHECKLIST**

| | |
|---|---|
| age 3–4+ | |
| outdoor | ✓ |
| no. of children | no limit |
| time | 10 minutes or more |
| help required | ✓ |
| no mess | ✓ |

**EQUIPMENT**
none required

### What the child learns
To be observant, to recognize letters and words, and to realize the many contexts in which letters and numbers are found. Also gives her counting practice.

# Easy Peasy

This is a simple rhyming game to play in odd moments. The task is to find a rhyme for a word—the sillier the combination, the better.

Encourage the child to find a rhyme for her daily activities: let's go walkie-talkie, bump and jump, into the far car, bark to the park.

Choose a few categories of things such as food items or clothes and make good silly rhymes: mean beans, bread in bed, butter in the gutter, and cat's hats.

# Counting out and about

**CHECKLIST**

age 3–4+

| | |
|---|---|
| outdoor | ✓ |
| no. of children | no limit |
| time | 10 minutes or more |
| help required | ✓ |
| no mess | ✓ |

**EQUIPMENT**

none required

## What the child learns

These games give a child confidence with numbers, which will get her off to a flying start. Mastering numbers and what they mean is a difficult task that needs lots of practice. Mathematics is logical and straightforward, and not inherently difficult—we usually fail at mathematics because we don't think we can do it; confidence is key.

Once a child can count, there are lots and lots of opportunities for you to practice with her. Here are just a few suggestions; you can probably think of many others yourself.

## what to do

How many people are at the bus stop?

How many children are on the bus?

How many dogs are tied up outside the shop?

How many trees have pink blossoms?

How many coins are needed to buy an ice cream cone?

How many steps does it take to pass the wall; to reach the mailbox; to go up the slide?

# Learning scrapbook

**CHECKLIST**

| | |
|---|---|
| age 3–6 | |
| indoor | ✓ |
| no. of children | no limit |
| time | can be spread over a few days |
| help required | ✓ |
| messy | ✓ |

**EQUIPMENT**

- good-quality scrapbook (make sure there are enough pages before you start, and divide up the pages if necessary)
- old newspapers, magazines, and mail-order catalogs
- scissors
- glue and brush
- felt-tipped pens

Bookstores are filled with counting and alphabet books for children, but it is still fun to make your own. Also, the message is much clearer when *he* has decided what object should be chosen for each letter.

## what to do

Think about each letter of the alphabet in turn and get the child to decide what to use for that page. Then help him look for suitable pictures.

For a number scrapbook, you need a smaller variety of pictures but more of each of them. Remember that the bigger numbers will take a lot of space, so use double page spreads for these and choose something he can find enough examples of, such as flowers found in seed catalogs.

## What the child learns

The alphabet, the sounds of the letters, and how they can be heard at the beginning of words. Numbers and the order of numbers. If you put three cars on page three, he will also learn to match the name with the quantity. Hand–eye coordination. Planning. Sitting still and "getting on with it." This is excellent practice for school.

# Teddy's tea party

CHECKLIST

| age 3–6 | |
| --- | --- |
| indoor/outdoor | ✓ |
| no. of children | no limit |
| time | 1–2 hours |
| help required | for younger children |
| not very messy | ✓ |

**EQUIPMENT**

- teddy bears, dolls, or stuffed animals
- tablecloth and low table (optional)
- paper towels, paper, and cardboard
- felt-tipped pens, pencils
- toy tea set (or old cups, plates, and saucers), cutlery
- food, either real or made from play dough

## What the child learns

To sort and match, to carry out a sustained activity, to start at the beginning and carry a task through to its end. To remember, think about, and prepare certain things in advance.

Setting the table is a repetitive sorting game that is more complex than sorting by color or size, as on page 47. For place settings, each person is given one of each object: one cup, one saucer, one knife, one fork, one spoon.

## what to do

Select a small table, such as a coffee table, for the tea party or put a cloth on the floor for a picnic.

Get the child to sit 3–4 teddy bears or dolls around the table, remembering to put bibs on the younger and messier ones (some paper towels tucked around their necks will do fine).

She can make little place mats from cardboard and decorate them with felt-tipped pens, make napkin holders from cutting the cardboard tube from an empty paper towel roll into sections, and write their names on little name tags using real or pretend writing.

She then sets out places for each of the toys using the mats, napkins, place names, cutlery, and her tea set.

She can pour each guest a pretend cup of tea and give them little cakes made from play dough.

She might even make them some tiny sandwiches and some real mini muffins (see page 64). Look for the little cases in the baking section of the supermarket to make teddy-bear-sized cakes!

# Just measuring

**CHECKLIST**

age 4–6

| | |
|---|---|
| indoor/outdoor | ✓ |
| no. of children | no limit |
| time | 10 minutes to half a day |
| help required | to start |
| no mess | ✓ |

**EQUIPMENT**

- dressmaker's tape measure
- metal tape measure
- ruler
- wall chart and pencil

## What the child learns

To work with and become familiar with numbers. A sense of what numbers mean, such as beginning to understand that six is a lot more than two but only a little more than five.

A child can spend many happy and productive hours measuring. How wide is the book? How long is his shoe? How many steps is it to the front door? This simple activity encourages him to work with numbers, reading them, saying their names, and gaining a sense of what numbers mean.

## what to do

Provide a cloth dressmaker's tape, a metal measuring tape, and a ruler and show the child how to use them. Encourage him to measure whatever he chooses: paving slabs, steps, the circumference of trees, and the length of his bed.

Make a wall chart and measure his height on it. Make a mark and date it. Repeat this every few months so that he can look back and measure how much he has grown.

Teach him how to measure in strides, arm lengths, and hands. It is all good practice for counting and adding.

# Weighing rice

This can be a simple or challenging task. Older children will enjoy filling in a work sheet. List the tasks to be carried out and leave a space for the child to put his answer on the sheet. He can write the answer, put a number of dots or lines, stick on a numbered label, or just put a star in the box when he has finished the task.

## what to do

How much does a full cup weigh? Fill a measuring cup with rice and then weigh it.

Does a cup of long-grain rice weigh as much as a cup of short-grain rice or lentils?

Pour a large bag of rice into a bowl. Use a measuring cup to fill a small breakfast bowl or a soup bowl. How many cups were needed?

How many spoonfuls of rice are needed to fill a cup?

**CHECKLIST**

| | |
|---|---|
| age 3+ | |
| indoor/outdoor | ✓ |
| no. of children | 1–3 |
| time | 30 minutes–1 hour |
| help required | ✓ |
| messy | ✓ |

**EQUIPMENT**
- rice (at least two kinds: long-grain and short-grain, or lentils)
- weighing scales (preferably one with two pans and separate weights)
- measuring cups and spoons
- selection of pitchers, mugs, and bowls
- paper and pens
- labels or adhesive stars (optional)

## What the child learns

Lots of straightforward mathematical skills here—he learns about volume, weight, numbers.

# Baby clinic

**CHECKLIST**

age 4–6

| | |
|---|---|
| indoor | ✓ |
| no. of children | no limit |
| time | 1 hour to half a day |
| help required | ✓ |
| no mess | ✓ |

**EQUIPMENT**

- record cards and pencils
- kitchen scales, preferably one with weights
- metal tape measure or ruler (try to find one with clear numbers)
- dolls, teddy bears, and stuffed animals
- doctor's kit (optional)

## What the child learns

To weigh and to measure. To learn about concepts such as big and small, heavy and light. To put things into sequence: this teddy is the heaviest, this one is the lightest, and so on. To carry out a sustained activity by starting at the beginning and carrying the task through to its end. To plan, remember, and prepare ahead of the game.

**This is another simple game that includes weighing and measuring as well as matching and pretending. The child plays at being the doctor while her stuffed animals, dolls, and teddy bears are the baby patients, so lots of talking is involved, too.**

## what to do

Before the game begins, the child can make a record card for each baby. The card should have baby's name, a place to record weight and length, and space for other comments. This is a good activity for you to do together on the computer.

Next, set up the clinic. She will need a pair of scales to weigh the babies. Pan scales with weights are best, but any scales with a pan or bowl to sit the patient in will do. She will also need a metal tape measure or ruler to measure how tall the babies are.

Let the examinations begin! Weigh each baby and measure its height. To see how tall it is, place a ruler or tape measure on the floor at right angles to a wall and lie the baby next to it with the top of its head against the wall. Put a card under the baby's feet and see where it comes to on the ruler or tape measure. Do not worry about fractions.

Record the findings on the record card, with assistance if necessary. If she has a doctor's kit, she could also listen to their chests, look at their tongues, and give them their injections.

Compare the results and arrange the babies in order of weight and height.

# Name that window

**CHECKLIST**

| | |
|---|---|
| age 3–4+ | |
| indoor | ✓ |
| no. of children | no limit |
| time | 10 minutes or more |
| help required | ✓ |
| no mess | ✓ |

**EQUIPMENT**
- index cards
- adhesive gum or tape
- paper and pen

## What the child learns
To begin to read simple words in context.

**This is not so much a game as a way of familiarizing children with the shapes of the written words for common objects.**

## what to do
Write the names of household structures or objects onto index cards (in lowercase letters), then stick the name card onto the object itself. For example, write "door" on one card and stick it onto the door, stick a "window" card onto the window, and so on. Choose about six names at a time and keep them in place for about a week, then choose another six and put them in place.

Write the words out on a big sheet of paper, remove all the word cards and see if the child can match the label to the words on the sheet. He will be able to do this as he begins to recognize the words. Begin by selecting words that have clearly different shapes—such as window and door—to make the task easier.

# In the bag

This simple activity draws children's attention to the beginning of a word. It is a form of the perennial favorite *I Spy*, but it is one that is easier on parents.

## what to do

Give the child a shopping bag, and tie a tag to it. Write a letter on the tag. The child then has to find five things starting with the letter to put into the bag. When you have checked that he has not made any mistakes, let him start with a new letter. Praise success and play down failures: "Wow, you got two right—and this letter's really hard!" To begin with, use the letters that only ever have one sound, such as b, d, or f, rather than those that can have two, such as c (can be pronounced as "k" or "s").

Modify the requirements according to each child's competence. You could progress to common combinations of letters, such as sh, ch, th, and so on. If it's hard to find five things for a particular letter or combination, reduce the number.

**CHECKLIST**

| | |
|---|---|
| age 4–6 | |
| indoor | ✓ |
| no. of children | no limit |
| time | 10 minutes or more |
| help required | ✓ |
| no mess | ✓ |

**EQUIPMENT**
- bag
- tags
- household objects

## What the child learns

To recognize letters, to see the relationship between a letter and a sound, and to hear the little sounds at the start of words.

# Let's cook together

**CHECKLIST**

age 3–6

| | |
|---|---|
| indoor | ✓ |
| no. of children | no limit |
| time | 1 hour |
| help required | ✓ |
| messy | ✓ |

**EQUIPMENT**

- cooking ingredients (see also pages 64–65)
- kitchen appliances and equipment

## What the child learns

To measure, chop, mix and count. To carry out an activity in an ordered way. To follow instructions. Confidence and a sense of achievement.

Cooking is science, it's mathematics, and it's a helping skill. It's also a way to gain pride in a simple achievement. Cooking is one of the few activities a child can undertake that produces an end product that looks as professional as her parents could produce.

## what to do

**SAFETY**

Although there are obvious dangers in the kitchen—hot ovens and very sharp knives—there are tasks that a child can do safely, such as measuring and cutting soft ingredients like bananas or mushrooms with a blunt knife. She will learn that it is fun to work together, and that being helpful and preparing things for the family does not have to be a chore.

Kitchen gadgets can extend the child's opportunities for joining in. A food processor allows her to chop ingredients under a watchful eye. A mixer allows her to make the sort of cakes that need beating—a task the under-sixes find difficult by hand. Easiest of all, a bread maker allows her to weigh out ingredients before going to bed, and wake up to her own bread for breakfast.

**WEIGHING AND MEASURING**

Wobbling scales are difficult to read. The easiest scale for a child to use is the old-fashioned balance. She selects the weights and puts them on one side and then carefully spoons the food into the pan on the other side. Measuring cups are even easier for a small child to use than scales.

## CHOPPING AND RIPPING

Let a small child cut soft food with a blunt knife. An older (and careful) child can use a cutting knife under instruction, but should never be left alone with it. Always select knives that have a rounded end rather than a point. Serrated knives are safer and easier for a child to use. Let her rip up leaves for salads.

## EASY JOBS FOR EVERYONE

Greasing pans, finding ingredients in the cupboard, and washing up afterward are all tasks a three-year-old will enjoy. Even a toddler can stir a cake.

# Making a frittata

**10 oz. (300 g) mushrooms, wiped**
**1 tablespoon olive oil**
**3½ oz. (110 g) Gruyère cheese**
**8 eggs**
**black pepper**
**salad ingredients**

Cut small mushrooms into four pieces and large ones into eight pieces. They are easy to cut with an ordinary knife, so let the child do it. Then (you) heat a teaspoon of the olive oil in a frying pan until it is very hot and add the mushrooms and stir for 1–2 minutes. Turn the heat down very low and let them cook for 5 minutes more. Shake the pan and stir it from time to time.

Meanwhile, let the child grate about a third of the cheese into a dish and cut the rest into tiny cubes. Then she should beat the eggs in a large bowl.

When the mushrooms are cooked, add them to the eggs together with the cubes of cheese. Season with black pepper. Wipe out the pan, then (you) add the rest of the oil. When it is hot, turn the heat down to the lowest possible setting and add the egg and mushroom mixture to the pan. Let the child quickly scatter the grated cheese on the top.

Heat the frittata for about 10 minutes. Preheat the oven broiler and, once it is hot, (you) place the pan under the broiler until the top has set—it should take less than a minute. While the frittata is cooking, your child can make a simple salad to go with it.

# What's for snack?

| | |
|---|---|
| age 4–6 | |
| indoor | ✓ |
| no. of children | 1–2 |
| time | 1 hour per recipe (excluding baking time) |
| help required | ✓ |
| messy | ✓ |

**EQUIPMENT**

- cooking ingredients (see each recipe)
- kitchen appliances and equipment

## What the child learns

To measure, count, chop, and mix. To carry out an activity in an ordered way. To follow instructions. Confidence and a sense of achievement.

As we saw in the previous activity, cooking is a helping skill and contains elements of science and mathematics. A child will really enjoy the measuring, weighing, and mixing involved in making cakes. Also important is the sense of achievement he gets from seeing (and eating!) a batch of cakes he has produced.

## what to do

**MUFFINS**

*1 cup (275 g) all-purpose flour*
*2 teaspoons double-acting baking powder*
*1 teaspoon salt*
*2 large eggs*
*½ cup (125 ml) milk*
*¼ cup (75 g) sugar*
*1 tablespoon (25 g) butter*

Add one or more of the following:

- 2 teaspoons ground cinnamon and ½ cup (115 g) raisins
- 3 large bananas, mashed, and a few pecan nuts
- 1 cup (250 g) fresh berries
- ½ cup (115 g) chocolate chips, and replace ¼ cup (75 g) of the flour with cocoa powder
- 1½ cups (325 g) sliced apple, plum, pear, or apricot
- 1 cup (200 g) grated carrot with the grated rind of 1 orange and ½ cup (75 g) nuts
- grated rind of 1 orange, and 1 tablespoon marmalade
- grated rind of 1 lemon, and 1 tablespoon lemon curd

Preheat the oven to 375°F/190°C/Gas Mark 5. Put 12 muffin cups in a muffin pan. Measure out all the ingredients, allowing the child to help wherever possible. Show him how to sift the flour and baking powder into a bowl and add the salt. When he has done this, put it aside.

Take a second larger bowl and break the eggs into it. Let him whisk them, adding the milk and then the sugar, while you melt the butter in a saucepan over a gentle heat. When it is melted, add it to the egg mixture and let him beat it again. If using bananas to flavor the muffins, mash them and add to the egg mixture.

So far the cake can be mixed with an electric beater or in a food processor, but the next part must be done by hand. Spoon the flour mixture onto the egg mixture and stir two or three times—*no more*. The flour should be disappearing but it should look very lumpy. Now add your extras, again stirring only twice.

Transfer the mixture to the muffin cups with a teaspoon; they should be two-thirds full. Bake in the preheated oven for 25 minutes. Remove and leave the muffins in the pan for about 5 minutes before transferring them to a wire rack to cool.

# Banana bread

**This is a quick-bread a five-year-old can make almost by himself.**

**3 ripe bananas**
**1 cup (250 g) sugar**
**¼ cup (75 g) oil**
**1 egg**
**1½ cups (325 g) all-purpose flour**
**1 teaspoon baking soda**
**1 teaspoon salt**
**1 teaspoon vanilla**
**½ cup (115 g) chopped walnuts (optional)**

Preheat the oven to 350°F/180°C/Gas Mark 4. Let the child start by mashing the bananas, measuring out the ingredients, greasing a loaf pan, and shaking some flour over the grease.

Now mix together the sugar and oil. The child can do this with a fork, or you can show him how to use an electric or hand beater. Mix in the egg and then add the flour, baking soda, salt, and vanilla. Finally, add the mashed bananas.

Put the mixture into the loaf pan and bake for 1 hour. To serve, cut in slices and spread with cream cheese.

# Tongue twisters

| | |
|---|---|
| age 4–6 | |
| indoor/outdoor | ✓ |
| no. of children | no limit |
| time | 10 minutes or more |
| help required | ✓ |
| no mess | ✓ |

**EQUIPMENT**

none required

## What the child learns

There is no better way to draw the child's attention to the little sounds that make up words.

Learning to read and spell is a complex process with many components. The one that causes most children problems is hearing the little sounds that make up words. Children with dyslexia have particular problems with this, but research shows that early practice can ease their problems. If dyslexia runs in your family (and it does tend to run in families), you should repeat these tongue twisters whenever you can. It does not matter whether the child tries to say the twisters or you make errors and he laughs, because it is what the child hears that is important.

## what to do

### Careful Katie

*Careful Katie cooked
    a crisp and crinkly
    cabbage.
Did careful Katie cook a
    crisp and crinkly
    cabbage?
If careful Katie cooked a
    crisp and crinkly
    cabbage,
where's the crisp and
    crinkly cabbage careful
    Katie cooked?*

### She sells seashells

*She sells seashells by the
    seashore.
The shells she sells are sea-
    shells, I'm sure.
So if she sells seashells by
    the seashore,
I'm sure that the shells are
    seashore shells.*

## Peter Piper

*Peter Piper picked a peck of pickled peppers;*
*A peck of pickled peppers Peter Piper picked;*
*If Peter Piper picked a peck of pickled*
*    peppers,*
*How many pickled peppers did Peter Piper*
*    pick?*

## Peggy Babcock

This is one that no one can say: just
repeat the name Peggy Babcock ten
times as fast as you can.

## Toy boat

Repeat this one as fast as you can,
ten times.

## Betty Botter

*Betty Botter bought some butter.*
*But she said the butter's bitter.*
*If I put it in my batter,*
*    it will make the batter bitter.*
*But a bit of better butter*
*    will make my batter better.*
*So she bought a bit of butter,*
*    better than her bitter butter,*
*    and she put it in her batter.*
*So 'twas better Betty Botter*
*    bought a bit of better butter.*

# A deck of cards

**CHECKLIST**

age 3–4+

| | |
|---|---|
| indoor | ✓ |
| no. of children | no limit |
| time | 10 minutes or more |
| help required | ✓ |
| messy | making the cards |

**EQUIPMENT**

- 2 decks of cards
- buttons, pasta shapes, and bowls
- 2 catalogs and postcards
- scissors
- paste

## What the child learns

Lots of mathematical skills here: matching, sorting, recognizing, and remembering. Encourages the child to look for detail, and it is good for spatial skills, too.

Most board games are difficult for small children, who are never sure which way to travel, have no idea of strategy, and get upset if they do not win. The general feeling is that if a preschooler is allowed to play, then adults and older children find it dull. Pairs is an exception. Because the preschooler's visual memory is considerably better than an adult's, her lack of strategy is compensated for by her ability to remember where something is.

## what to do

### PAIRS

Take two identical decks of playing cards and select the following cards from each pack: 1, 5, and 10 of hearts; 2, 6, and jack of spades; 3, 7, and queen of clubs; and 4, 8, and king of diamonds. Place these face down on the table.

The first person turns over two cards. If they are the same, she takes them; if not, she turns them back and the next person takes a turn. The skill is in remembering where each of the cards are. When all the pairs have been found, the game starts again.

The game can be made easier by using fewer pairs, harder by using more. You can also use picture cards, available from most toy stores, or you can make your own (see panel, right).

### LOTTO

This game is also played with two decks of cards. Put one deck in the middle of the table. From the other deck, deal 4–9 cards face up in front of each player.

Players take turns to turn over a card from the deck in the middle. If one of them matches one of her cards she takes it and places it on top of her own card, face down. The game continues until the first player covers all her cards.

### COUNT IT

Deal out the 2, 4, 5, and 6 of hearts. Give the child a bag of buttons and let her put one button over each heart. If

you can find some heart-shaped buttons, so much the better.

Put a small bowl in front of each card. Give the child a bigger bowl of pasta shapes (bows or shells, for example) and let her count the correct number (as on each card) into each small bowl.

### SORT IT

Give the child a deck of cards and let her sort them into suits.

Can she sort the deck into numbers? This is much harder to do, so take out the higher numbers if she finds it too difficult.

### JIGSAWS

Take cards numbered 1–4, each number in a different suit. Cut the 2 in half, the 3 into thirds, the 4 in quarters. Let her put the pieces back together again.

# To make picture cards

**Buy a package of blank index cards. Cut each card in half and stick the two halves together to make a stiff card. Pick up two copies of a catalog from a store selling household items or toys. Cut out identical pictures of familiar items such as a refrigerator, TV, bed, or chair from each catalog and stick them onto the cards.**

* Spectacular plants to grow
* Beans in a jar
* How plants grow
* Spiky monsters!
* Games with mirrors
* Attract-magnets
* Magic scribble pad
* Invisible ink
* Let's make lollipops!
* A spoonful of baking soda
* Grand sand
* Good vibrations
* Slug walk
* Catching insects
* Under a stone
* City wildlife
* Since records began
* Bird table
* Nature table
* Animal tracks and trails

Science

and nature

# Spectacular plants to grow

**EQUIPMENT**

- seeds
- plant pots
- compost
- trowel, rake, and bulb planter (easier for a child to dig a hole with than a spade)
- watering can or hose

## What the child learns

How things grow and change, how to plan and work toward a long-term goal. To have patience. Pride when his first crop of vegetables is harvested.

Small children do not have the patience to wait for months to see if a plant will grow, so always look at the germination time before buying seeds for them. Flowers and vegetables that mature within weeks of sowing are best, or look for large annual climbers and sunflowers that have to get a move on! See also Spiky monsters! (growing mustard and cress), page 77, and Beans in a jar, page 74.

## what to do

### SELECTING AND SOWING SEEDS

Find the child a little corner of the garden or a pot on the terrace. Pots are good for small children to garden in because they can get to the weeds without any danger of stepping on their plants. Pots do, however, need regular and generous watering (which is not necessarily a bad thing).

Select the seeds. Try radishes, which mature within weeks; carrots (the little plants are easy to pick out); or sunflowers, which are easy to sow and grow at spectacular rates.

Prepare the ground. Weeds always seem to come up faster than even the fastest crop, so you may find it easier to grow your first batch of seeds in potting compost. That way you can be sure that everything that germinates is the child's.

Help him to prepare the seed rows. Mark the lines with a stick and let him sow the seeds and cover them with compost. This helps him to see where the seeds are.

Mix fine seeds with a little sand or compost to make them easier to sow.

Water frequently, but don't soak the ground too much.

# Good plants for children to grow

Rhubarb makes a spectacular plant. A couple of crowns will soon fill a corner of the garden, and the child can help you make a crumble or a rhubarb fool with the produce. **Be warned,** however: The leaves are poisonous, so be sure he doesn't eat them and always wash his hands after he has handled them.

The child could have his own grow bag of tomatoes, or, if space is really limited, look for the varieties you can grow in hanging baskets.

Potatoes can be grown in a pot. Look for kits at garden centers.

Strawberries make excellent pot plants.

Check out salad greens that you harvest a few leaves at a time.

A fruit tree on small stock could grow up with the child, giving years of pleasure and interest.

# Beans in a jar

**EQUIPMENT**

- jar
- dried beans or peas
- thread
- blotting paper
- adhesive tape
- rubber band

## What the child learns

This is probably the best possible way for a child to see how roots and shoots emerge from a seed.

This is a simple demonstration of how things grow. You will probably need to set this up for the child, and a certain amount of patience is needed while you wait for the beans to sprout. Set it up at the start of a busy week or before going away for a few days. Things will start to happen quite quickly as soon as you have the time to watch.

## what to do

First soak the beans overnight. Then attach threads to them. It is easier to do this with big beans but possible with smaller beans and even peas.

Prepare your jar: Make a roll of blotting paper about 4–5 layers thick. It should fit neatly against the glass, so cut it to size before you put it in the jar. Check that it fits and then remove it.

Hang your soaked beans by their threads inside the jar. Secure the threads to the top of the jar with adhesive tape so that they rest about halfway down. When you have them all hanging in place (you should have room for 4–5 in a jam jar), wrap a rubber band around the neck of the jar to make sure the threads stay in place.

Now put the blotting paper back into the jar, taking care not to disturb the beans too much. They should be suspended between the glass and just touching the blotting paper.

Pour water into the jar. There should be some left in the base of the jar after the blotting paper has soaked it up, but the beans should not be submerged.

Always ensure that the blotting paper remains wet and that the beans remain in contact with it. Wait. Once the beans sprout, the child can watch the roots and shoots develop. Make sure that the beans get plenty of light once they start to grow.

It's fun to watch the shoots popping out of the bean and the roots growing down—but better still to grow the plants and harvest the beans.

Once the beans have sprouted, carefully remove most of them and pot them in compost (or better still, in the garden) and water them carefully. They should produce a crop of beans within a few months.

Take one of the beans that has sprouted and carefully unpeel the skin. Look at the two halves of the bean. Can you see where the growth starts?

# How plants grow

**CHECKLIST**

| | |
|---|---|
| age 5–6 | |
| indoor/outdoor | ✓ |
| no. of children | no limit |
| time | 10 minutes or more |
| help required | ✓ |
| no mess | ✓ |

**EQUIPMENT**

- plants
- pots
- compost
- water

## What the child learns

To be observant. To ask questions and discover the answers.

Children will enjoy the following simple experiments to show that plants seek light and need water.

## what to do

**PLANTS SEEK LIGHT**

Look at the way houseplants grow toward the window. In the garden, look at how plants in shady areas bend over toward the light.

Plant some Impatiens in two pots. Put one pot in a dark cupboard and the other in the sunshine. Check both every few days to see what has happened.

**PLANTS NEED WATER**

Look at what happens to plants in the garden when it is hot and dry. Look at what happens to houseplants if they are not watered.

Water plants that are drooping before you go shopping; then take a look at them as soon as you get home.

# Spiky monsters!

Growing mustard and cress on an old sponge or some damp absorbent cotton is a favorite with preschool children. Making monsters with cress "spikes" is a fun variation on this theme.

## what to do

Take a baking potato about the size of a serving spoon and scoop a hole into the top of it.

Poke four spent matchsticks into the underside of the potato (underneath) to make the legs.

Make eyes and nose from round head thumbtacks—the kind used to identify places on a wall map.

Now fill the hole with damp cotton and sow mustard seeds, cress seeds, or a mixture of the two, liberally.

Stand the "monster" in a warm sunny spot and wait! Shoots will appear within just a few days.

When it has grown, make the cress into a sandwich with some scrambled egg and mayonnaise.

CHECKLIST

| age 3–6 | |
| --- | --- |
| indoor | ✓ |
| no. of children | no limit |
| time | about 1 hour |
| help required | ✓ |
| no mess | ✓ |

EQUIPMENT
• baking potatoes
• matchsticks
• round head thumbtacks
• absorbent cotton
• mustard or cress seeds

## What the child learns

That seeds grow into plants that can be eaten. That seeds need water and light to grow. This is a delightful way to grow a crop of mustard and cress for a sandwich, and will appeal to children who do not otherwise enjoy growing things.

# Games with mirrors

CHECKLIST

age 3–4+

| | |
|---|---|
| indoor/outdoor | ✓ |
| no. of children | no limit |
| time | 10 minutes to half a day |
| help required | ✓ |
| no mess | ✓ |

EQUIPMENT

- mirrors of various sizes
- dice or other small object
- mirror tiles and adhesive tape
- chopstick, mug, and plastic bottle
- different colored sheets of acetate, flashlight, powder paints
- paper towel or toilet paper tubes, pair of drinking glasses, stick, glass of water

## What the child learns

This series of simple experiments teaches the child in an informal way about the reflection of light. Explain to her that when light falls on a surface it is usually "swallowed up" but that mirrors bounce it all back the way it came. These sorts of science experiments encourage careful and systematic observation, a skill needed in many aspects of school work.

Children can keep themselves amused for hours experimenting with a small mirror. Use a mirror with a backing. A compact or hand mirror is ideal. For the youngest children, use a baby mirror or a metal mirror tile with the edges bound in tape.

## what to do

Catch the sun in a small hand mirror and play the reflection over the wall.

Put a dice or other small object in front of the mirror, then move it back. The dice in the mirror will move back by the same amount.

Encourage the child to look at her reflection in a still pool, and see how the trees are reflected, too. What happens when she throws a stone in the water?

Write her name and hold it up to the mirror. What happens?

Get her to try to put a chopstick into a mug by watching the reflection in the dressing table mirror. If that proves easy, put a plastic bottle in one hand and the chopstick in the other and try to get the chopstick into the neck of the bottle.

If you have a dressing table with three mirrors, set it up to get multiple reflections. If not, buy three mirror tiles and use wide tape to make a line of three. Now let her look at her many reflections.

If you have a closet door with a mirror, stand the child at the edge of the door and get her to lift her feet up. It looks like both feet are off the ground!

Get the child to look at herself in the door mirror. What happens to the background if you move the door?

# World of colors

The world looks different when you look at it through tinted acetate. When you mix colored lights, the result is different from mixing paints because what we see when we look at a painted surface is a reflection of that light. What we see when we look through acetate is the light itself.

Cut small squares of different colored acetate and encourage her to look through them.

Shine a flashlight through the acetate to make colored lights.

Shine a flashlight beam through combinations of colors.

Mix paints of the same color. Do they act in the same way?

# A different view

Science is about exploration—looking for how things change and whether there are constants in the world. Looking at things from a different angle is the simplest form of investigation for a very young child. Encourage her to:

Look through a paper towel or toilet paper tube. Then look through two.

Look through a pair of drinking glasses.

Look at a stick in water through the side of a glass.

**Science and nature**

# Attract-magnets

**CHECKLIST**

| | |
|---|---|
| age 3+ | |
| indoor | ✓ |
| no. of children | no limit |
| time | 30 minutes–2 hours |
| no help required | ✓ |
| not very messy | ✓ |

**EQUIPMENT**

- magnet or pair of magnets
- small metal objects such as paper clips, cutlery, and toys

## What the child learns

This is a simple science task a child can carry out by himself. It will give him both confidence and enjoyment. It teaches him to ask questions and find answers.

Magnets delight small children because they can use them to carry out their own investigations with little interference from adults. They love watching things jump onto the poles of the magnet and feeling the force of the poles pushing apart.

## what to do

Let the child see which objects the magnet will stick to. Try the refrigerator and washing machine, the bath, door handles, trays, and various toys.

Let him use the magnet to lift small objects.

Investigate what happens when two magnets are pushed together. What happens if one of the magnets is turned around or, if they are horseshoe magnets, if one is turned over?

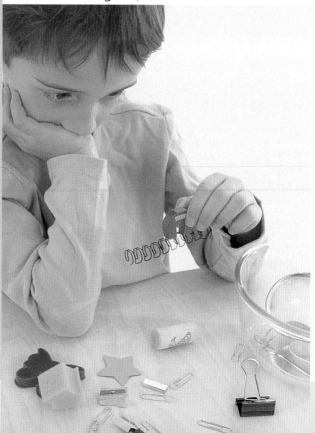

# Magic scribble pad

Children love the "now you see it, now you don't" element of these magic pads, which are surprisingly easy to make. Making your own allows you to make them as big or as small as you like.

## what to do

Take a sheet of cardboard. Place a sheet of carbon paper—carbon side up—on top of this and secure with tape. This can be a bit difficult and most children will need help. They do not need to seal all the edges, just enough to hold the paper firmly in place.

Next, cover the carbon paper—first with waxed paper and then with a layer of cellophane or a very thin sheet of clear plastic. The last two layers are secured across the top only; use tape and staples for this.

Draw on the pad. Erase by lifting the two top layers.

**CHECKLIST**

age 3–4+

| indoor | ✓ |
|---|---|
| no. of children | no limit |
| time | 10 minutes or more |
| help required | ✓ |
| no mess | ✓ |

**EQUIPMENT**
- piece of cardboard
- carbon paper
- waxed paper
- cellophane or clear plastic
- adhesive tape and staples

## What the child learns
To plan and carry out a task in an ordered way. Making something he enjoys playing with gives him pride and self-confidence.

# Invisible ink

**CHECKLIST**

| | |
|---|---|
| age 3–4+ | |
| indoor | ✓ |
| no. of children | no limit |
| time | 30 minutes or more |
| help required | ✓ |
| messy | ✓ |

**EQUIPMENT**

- wax candles and wax crayons
- paper
- water-soluble paint, paintbrush
- potato juice or lemon juice
- margarine

## What the child learns

That oil and water do not mix. Once she knows this, there are lots of ways she can check this out. Look for oil on puddles, mix cooking oil with water, and see how fat sets on the top of stock as it cools.

It's magic, and it's science, too. Water runs off wax. You can show children how this works by rubbing a block of margarine over half a sheet of newspaper and then splashing it with water. The margarine stops the water from soaking into the paper. Ducks keep water out of their feathers by the same principle.

## what to do

Cover a sheet of paper with candle-wax scribbles. Put it face down on top of a second sheet of paper, and write a message on the top sheet. To reveal the message, paint over the top of the lower sheet of paper.

The child could write the message using the candle like a crayon and then paint the page to reveal it in the same way.

Potato juice or lemon juice can be used to write a message. Just warm it in the oven when it is time to read it.

Get the child to draw secret pictures using candle wax and try to guess what they are (or the other way around). All is revealed when she paints over the wax. She can achieve the same effect using crayons or a block of margarine, although not so secretively.

**WARNING**
When putting paper in the oven, make sure the temperature is set very low and do not leave unattended. The adult, not the child, should put the paper in the oven.

# Let's make lollipops!

Lollipops are easy to make, and a home-made lollipop is a lot healthier (and cheaper) than a bought one. Making something for themselves is a very positive experience for children.

## what to do

You will need a set of plastic lollipop molds or small paper cups, some sticks (plastic stirrers would work well; tie two together if they seem a little thin), and some fruit juice.

Pour some juice into a smaller container—do not overfill it—and show the child how to pour it carefully into the mold.

Put the molds in the freezer. Once frozen, let her eat the lollipops.

Mini lollipops can be made in ice cube trays.

| CHECKLIST | |
| --- | --- |
| age 2–6 | |
| indoor | ✓ |
| no. of children | no limit |
| time | 15 minutes or more |
| help required | ✓ |
| messy | ✓ |

### EQUIPMENT
- plastic lollipop molds (from kitchen supply or department stores), small paper cups, or ice cube trays
- sticks made from plastic stirrers (the molds usually have their own)
- fruit juice and small container, preferably with a spout

## What the child learns
That liquid freezes when chilled. To make something she likes; to feel proud of what she achieves.

# A spoonful of baking soda

age 3–4+

| indoor/outdoor | ✓ |
| --- | --- |
| no. of children | no limit |
| time | 10 minutes–1 hour (not including cooking time) |
| help required | ✓ |
| messy | ✓ |

**EQUIPMENT**

- baking soda (available from the baking section of the supermarket)
- vinegar (or another acid such as lemon juice)
- plastic bottle with cork
- cake ingredients
- kitchen equipment and appliances

## What the child learns

This is simple science with the fastest possible result! The child learns about conducting experiments and about chemical reactions between an acid substance and an alkaline substance. Baking a cake teaches measuring and following instructions as well as creating a sense of achievement.

This demonstrates a simple but spectacular chemical reaction, which will blow out a cork (with careful supervision it is completely safe) and raise a cake. Vinegar is an acid. When it reacts with carbon it forms the gas carbon dioxide. It is these bubbles that escape with force in Fizz and Pop below. Cooking traps the bubbles, making cakes lighter.

## what to do

FIZZ!
Dissolve 1 teaspoon of baking soda in a little water, then add 3 tablespoons of vinegar. Stand back and watch it bubble up.

POP!
Fill a small plastic bottle three-quarters full with water and add 1 teaspoon of baking soda to every cup (300 ml) of water. Find a cork that fits the bottle (wrap paper around the cork to make a snug fit). Shake the bottle well. Remove the cork and take 3 tablespoons of vinegar (measure it into a separate container first) and pour it in. Quickly wedge in the cork. Stand well back and wait for it to pop.

**WARNING**
Never use a glass bottle, and do not be tempted to use more baking soda than suggested here.

# Raise a fruitcake

2 cups (500 g) plain flour
1 cup (250 g) brown sugar
1 cup (250 g) butter or margarine (cold)
fruit (see right for options)
1 cup (300 ml) milk
1 teaspoon baking soda
3 tablespoons vinegar

**FRUIT OPTIONS**
*choose one of the following:*
1 cup (250 g) seedless raisins
1 cup (250 g) chopped pears or apples
1 cup (250 g) chopped pineapple chunks
1 cup (250 g) grated carrots
2 mashed bananas

Preheat the oven to 400°F/200°C/Gas Mark 6. Thoroughly grease a round 9-inch cake pan and dust with flour. With the child's help, weigh and mix together the flour and brown sugar.

Cube the butter or margarine and add to the flour and sugar. Either mix in the food processor, or help the child rub the butter into the dry ingredients by hand. Add the fruit chosen from the options listed above.

Pour the milk into a 2-cup container and add a teaspoon of baking soda. Mix well. Measure 3 tablespoons of vinegar into a small cup and add this to the milk. It will froth up dramatically. Count to five, then pour the foaming milk into the cake mix. Stir in quickly and transfer to the greased cake pan.

Bake for 1 hour, then reduce the temperature to 325°F/160°C/Gas Mark 3, and bake for 1½ hours.

# Grand sand

**CHECKLIST**

| | |
|---|---|
| age 2+ | |
| outdoor | ✓ |
| no. of children | no limit |
| time | 30 minutes or more |
| no help required | ✓ |
| messy | ✓ |

**EQUIPMENT**

- play sand
- funnel, colander, strainers
- assorted containers, bowls, and cups
- bags
- water wheel
- pail and shovel
- flowers, twigs, stones
- loaf pan
- toy vehicles

## What the child learns

Lots of straightforward mathematical skills and simple science. Playing with sand encourages children to ask "why?"

There is nothing quite like sand. When it's dry it flows like water; when it's damp it molds like clay; and when it's really wet it flows like mud to make eerie shapes and fairy castles. Buy play sand because builder's sand is sharp and unpleasant to handle, and it is dirty and sticky.

## what to do

### DRY SAND

Give the child a bowl of dry sand, a funnel, a cup, a colander, and fine and coarse strainers and let her explore.

Give her an assortment of containers, bowls, and cups and ask her to find out which holds the most sand.

Fill a bag with dry sand, cut the corner off the bag and let the child "draw" with the stream of sand.

Make a little hill of sand and add the dry sand to the top. Watch how it rolls down the sides.

Buy a water wheel and pour the sand through it.

### WET SAND

Give the child a pail and shovel and let her build a castle.

Decorate with flowers, twigs, and small stones.

Fill a bag with semiliquid sand and cut the corner off. Use the stream to "draw" eerie shapes all over the construction.

Use the back of the shovel to draw roads through the sand and drive her cars through them. Use a loaf pan to construct buildings alongside the roads.

Scrape out an area of flat sand and draw in it (or write her name) with a stick.

# Good vibrations

**CHECKLIST**

| | |
|---|---|
| age 4–6 | |
| indoor | ✓ |
| no. of children | no limit |
| time | 10 minutes |
| help required | ✓ |
| not very messy | ✓ |

**EQUIPMENT**

- sheets of plastic, foil, and/or rubber
- bowl
- rubber band
- rice or sugar
- chopstick

## What the child learns

To carry out a simple investigation. To work systematically toward an end. To be observant.

When a drum skin is hit, it vibrates, and that vibration moves through the air. We hear this vibration as sound. It is not always possible to see the vibration, but we can demonstrate it by showing how the vibration causes other objects to move.

## what to do

Stretch a sheet of plastic or foil across the top of a bowl and fix it in place with a rubber band.

Put some grains of rice or sugar on top of the plastic or foil.

Tap the surface gently with a chopstick. Watch the rice jump up and down as the surface vibrates.

If you can, try a more elastic surface, such as rubber, to show that the vibrations last longer.

# Slug walk

This is a quick and simple watching activity that can keep small children amused for a surprisingly long period of time. Slugs and snails move on slime trails using little bumps called pseudopodia, a word that children often find funny.

## what to do

Collect slugs or snails from the garden; they are easy to find first thing in the morning or after it has rained.

Take a large sheet of clear acrylic and place it across two chairs. The child needs to lie on the floor and look up, so provide cushions so she can get a really close look.

Place the slugs or snails on top of the acrylic and wait for them to move. A drop of beer or a little lettuce might encourage them to move.

The child can also put them on a windowpane and look through the window at the underside of their bodies to see how they move.

**CHECKLIST**

| | |
|---|---|
| age 4–6 | |
| indoor/outdoor | ✓ |
| no. of children | no limit |
| time | 10 minutes or more |
| help required | ✓ |
| no mess | apart from slime trails |

**EQUIPMENT**
- snails and slugs
- acrylic sheet
- 2 dining chairs
- pillows
- nature books

## What the child learns
Careful observation of nature. Follow up by looking for nature books with information on slugs and snails for you to read together.

# Catching insects

**CHECKLIST**

| | |
|---|---|
| age 3–6 | |
| outdoor | ✓ |
| no. of children | no limit |
| time | 30 minutes–1 hour |
| help required | ✓ |
| no mess | ✓ |

**EQUIPMENT**

- screw-top jar
- sheet or pillowcase
- garden or park for plants with insects

## What the child learns

To be observant, to look for details. To plan and carry out an activity to fruition. To see how quickly the lives of small creatures pass.

Although it can be hard to find mice or other small mammals in the garden, there are always plenty of insects to discover and study. Even though they are small, it is easy to get in close and watch them.

## what to do

Put a pillowcase or an old sheet under a bush in the garden and have a glass jar with a screw top ready. Get the child to shake the bush—quite a few insects should fall down for him to collect.

Help him to put them in the jar and seal it. Get him to watch the insects he has caught. What color are they? How many legs have they got? Have they got wings? Can he see their eyes? If he intends to keep the insects overnight, make some air holes in the lid and give them a few damp leaves so they can eat and drink.

Look on rosebushes, broad beans, and nasturtiums for ladybugs or other beetles. He could pick a leaf that has very few of the tiny creatures on it and put the leaf (and a drop or two of water) in the jar. Make a few small holes in the lid. Add a new leaf and a few drops of water every day. How many bugs has he got by the end of the week?

# Under a stone

**CHECKLIST**

age 3–6

| | |
|---|---|
| outdoor | ✓ |
| no. of children | no limit |
| time | 1–2 hours |
| help required | for identification |
| no mess | ✓ |

**EQUIPMENT**
- reference book

## What the child learns
That he can find interesting things if he looks in the right places. Careful observation of detail for identification (a skill he needs for later reading). An appreciation that nature should not be disturbed. That creatures should be left to live their lives and for others to enjoy as he has done.

Some gardens do not have snails, and it can sometimes be hard to find ladybugs in the park. Do not despair, as one thing is certain: You will almost always find some small, many-legged creatures under a stone.

## what to do
Turn over a stone and watch the creatures scurrying out of the light. Look at the variety of creatures the child finds. Count them and try to study them.

Put the stone back carefully so the insects can return to normal, and turn over another one. Buy a reference book and find out what they are all called. Check off the ones he has seen.

# City wildlife

**CHECKLIST**

| | |
|---|---|
| age 3–4+ | |
| outdoor | ✓ |
| no. of children | no limit |
| time | 10 minutes or more |
| help required | ✓ |
| no mess | ✓ |

**EQUIPMENT**

none required

## What the child learns

Another task that encourages careful observation and encourages the child to be aware of the natural world.

It can be very difficult to see wildlife in the countryside because country animals are usually shy and not used to seeing people. City animals by contrast are used to people and are consequently much more bold.

## what to do

Go in search of wildlife. Underground and subway stations are probably the easiest places to see mice. You may be lucky enough to see a fox in the city, particularly near railway lines. Listen for their strange mating cry in the spring. Many parks and gardens have frogs and squirrels.

Birds often fly into the city at night to roost. If you know the roosting spots, make a visit at dusk to hear them squabbling over windowsills. Pigeons roost under bridges, leaving their telltale droppings, so it's easy to find them; go and visit at dusk. Most city ponds and rivers have ducks. In spring look for swallows, and at night look out for bats.

# Since records began

This is the hottest/wettest/snowiest day since records began. Today there are fewer/more birds at the bird table than yesterday, more yellow flowers, more daisies on the lawn, more trees with blossoms in the park (or whatever else the child would like to record) *since records began*. Although there are other reasons to keep records, small children like to know the best and the worst cases!

## what to do

Help the child decide what to record and when to record it. Get a small notebook to keep the records in and mark it up together.

Make the observation and record it in the book. An easy way to count when out for a walk is to have some buttons or coins in one pocket and switch them to another pocket or a small bag each time something needs to be counted. He can then do the real counting when you get home.

**CHECKLIST**

| | |
|---|---|
| age 3–6 | |
| outdoor | ✓ |
| no. of children | no limit |
| time | 10 minutes or more |
| help required | ✓ |
| no mess | ✓ |

**EQUIPMENT**
- notebook
- pencil
- buttons or small coins to count with

## What the child learns

To make plans and carry out a task systematically. To count. To observe carefully. Keeping records helps him to remember what he did and acts as a focus for conversation.

# Bird table

CHECKLIST

age 3–6

| | |
|---|---|
| indoor/outdoor | ✓ |
| no. of children | no limit |
| time | 10 minutes or more |
| help required | ✓ |
| messy | bird pudding only |

EQUIPMENT

- bird table
- bird food
- notebook and pencil
- for bird pudding: seeds, breadcrumbs, suet, nuts, dried fruit, meat, lard, string, yogurt container

## What the child learns

To pay attention and watch carefully. To keep records. To plan and do things in the correct order. To follow instructions.

Birds like to be in the open (whereas most small mammals run for cover), which makes them easier to watch. Most of the birds that visit city gardens have learned to be tolerant of people until they come really close.

## what to do

### FEED THE BIRDS

Set up a bird table where the child can view it from the window. Put a variety of food on the table to attract different birds. Some birds eat only seeds, others eat insects and worms, and some prefer tiny bits of meat. In winter, birds need fat, so offer them suet or a bird pudding (see panel opposite).

In winter, treat the birds to a block of creamed coconut (grated or chopped; check Indian or Middle Eastern grocers). You can also use it instead of lard in a bird pudding.

Encourage an older child to keep a record in a notebook of how many birds were at the table at different times of day and what they all ate.

# Make a bird pudding

Get a large mixing bowl and into it put a variety of seeds, some breadcrumbs, chopped suet, nuts, dried fruit, and some little bits of meat, such as bacon. Let the child mix all this together.

Now you melt some lard so it is just liquid but not too hot and pour this over the seed mixture. The mixture must be kneaded. Check that it is not too hot and show the child how to knead it. Be warned: It is very messy!

Loosely pack the lard and seed mixture into a yogurt container. Push a string down through the center and then press the mixture down so it is tightly packed around the string, adding more mixture if necessary. Let it harden, then turn it out and hang it up for the birds. Squirrels love this, too, but are inclined to run off with the whole pudding.

# Nature table

**CHECKLIST**

age 4+

| | |
|---|---|
| indoor/outdoor | ✓ |
| no. of children | no limit |
| time | 30 minutes–2 hours |
| help required | ✓ |
| no mess | ✓ |

**EQUIPMENT**

- nature table or tray for her collections
- bag for collecting items
- reference books
- pen, pencils, and crayons
- paper
- masking tape
- envelope to carry rubbings in

## What the child learns

This systematic activity has many learning opportunities: Children learn good pen control, enjoyment of nature, naming, writing, and reading, and how books can be used to gain useful information.

Children like to gather things when they are out and about. Always put a plastic bag in your pocket before you leave the house so you can carry these treasures home. At home, arrange them on a nature table, identify them, and write out labels for them.

## what to do

### COLLECT SPECIMENS

Encourage the child to pick up leaves, cones, nuts, fruit, berries, seed heads, and fallen blossoms (don't pick flowers—it's often illegal).

Collect the treasures in a bag and take them home.

Arrange them on a table or shelf. (If you cannot spare a dedicated table, use a tray.)

Identify what has been found, using reference books where necessary.

Help the child write labels if she is old enough. If not, you can write the date and what she has found, and she can do some "scribble writing" underneath. An older child can also copy what you have written on the label.

# Make bark rubbings

Take along a few small sheets of paper, some masking tape, and a soft pencil. Let the child choose a tree and stick the paper to the trunk at her height. Get her to gently scribble from left to right using a soft pencil or a crayon. Take a leaf from the tree to help you identify it.

Repeat on a different tree. Put the bark rubbings in an envelope for safekeeping until you get home. Rubbings can also be made from the leaves once you get home.

# Animal tracks and trails

**CHECKLIST**

| | |
|---|---|
| age 5–6 | |
| outdoor | ✓ |
| no. of children | no limit |
| time | 30 minutes–3 hours |
| help required | ✓ |
| no mess | ✓ |

**EQUIPMENT**

- reference book
- cardboard strips
- staples or paper clips
- plaster of paris

## What the child learns

To be observant. To look for and recognize small differences that help identify the tracks, a skill that is good preparation for reading.

The best places to search for animal tracks and signs are on soft ground, at the edge of water, on the beach, in snow, and in muddy damp spots. You do not need to live in the country, but you will probably find a larger variety of tracks if you do. In town, most of the footprints you'll find belong to people and their pets.

## what to do

Start by looking for the most obvious footprints. Those belonging to people, horses, ducks, and cows are all quite distinctive, and you can often tell who made them because they are still nearby.

On a beach or in the snow, bird tracks are easy to find, so are dog and cat tracks. Follow them. If you are lucky you will see how the pattern changes when animals move at a different pace or when birds take off or cats jump onto walls.

On the beach, check out how different your tracks look when you walk and when you run or jump.

Sometimes as you follow footprints you can find other signs that animals have passed by, such as broken branches, grass trodden down, even bits of fur caught up in a branch.

Tracks in a muddy area tell you it may be worth coming back at dusk to see if there are animals around.

Make plaster casts of footprints (see panel right). Then try and identify them using reference books, if necessary.

# Making a plaster cast of a footprint

**Clear away any loose dirt, leaves, or twigs from around the footprint. The ground must be quite dry for the cast to set.**

**Take 2-in. (5-cm) cardboard strips and fit them together around the footprint with staples or paper clips to make an upright frame.**

**Mix the plaster of paris with water to make a thick cream.**

**Carefully pour this into the footprint and the cardboard frame to a depth of about ½ in. (1 cm).**

**Let it set for a couple of hours until it is hard.**

**Remove the cardboard and lift the cast very carefully.**

# whatever

- Windy day
- Measuring the wind
- Windy day collage
- Wind chimes
- Parachutes
- Wishing tree
- Blowing bubbles
- Raindrop pictures
- Little boats
- Making a rain gauge
- Watching raindrops
- Making a weather chart
- Rainbows
- A walk in the rain
- A big happy sun picture
- Making a sundial
- Sunshine and shadows
- Snowstorm
- Making a snow scene
- A snowy day

the weather

# Windy day

**CHECKLIST**

| | |
|---|---|
| age 2+ | |
| outdoor | ✓ |
| no. of children | no limit |
| time | as long as the interest remains |
| help required | ✓ |
| no mess | ✓ |

**EQUIPMENT**

- a windy day!
- paper
- balloon and rice
- kite
- objects such as tissue paper, cork, screws

## What the child learns

The child learns about cause and effect, observational skills, and attention to detail. Outings like these also provide experiences to talk about, to use in pictures and collages and pretend games.

Wind excites children and puts them in the mood to learn. You will find they need very little encouragement. Because the wind changes the way things look and feel, there are lots of novel things to see and do. Remember that small children lose heat and that wind draws heat away from the body more quickly, so do not stay out too long on a wet or cold day.

## what to do

What flies? A paper plane will fly even without the wind, but it is much more dramatic on a windy day. For how to make a paper airplane, see page 167.

A balloon jiggles and struggles to get free in the wind (so attach it to the child to avoid it blowing away). Add some rice to the balloon before blowing it up to alter the way it moves.

A kite is difficult for a small child to control, but she can hold it for a while once you have launched it.

Watch how the wind makes ripples on the pond, or even a puddle.

Make a paper boat (see panel opposite) and watch how it sails away.

On the beach, watch the spray lifting off the top of the waves.

Check out what will blow away (and be sure to pick up everything afterward). Try little bits of tissue paper, a candy wrapper, a cork, some foil, a feather, some paper plates and cups, and maybe something heavier such as a screw or a ball. Does the shape matter?

## How to make a paper boat

Look for weather vanes. If you live near an airport, look for a wind sock. Can the child make one?

Listen to the noises the wind causes. Flapping laundry, rustling leaves, banging gates, and whistling around buildings.

Stand in a space where the child can open her arms and catch the wind. This is best if she has a nice wide flapping raincoat!

On a really windy day find the highest point you can and just stand there leaning into the wind!

Make a paper boat to float on a pond or in a puddle and watch how the wind blows it along. Follow the instructions in the panel (right), open out the paper into a boat, and it is ready to sail!

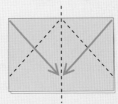

1. Fold a sheet of paper in half.

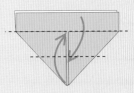

2. Fold in half again and then unfold.

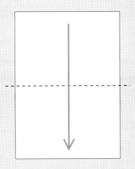

3. Fold the top corners down to the center crease, then rotate the paper 180 degrees.

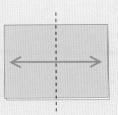

4. Fold the bottom point up. Then, fold top flap down, turn over, and repeat.

# Measuring the wind

**CHECKLIST**

| | |
|---|---|
| age 3–4+ | |
| outdoor | ✓ |
| no. of children | no limit |
| time | 10 minutes or more |
| help required | ✓ |
| no mess | ✓ |

**EQUIPMENT**

- scale to record the strength of the wind
- compass
- streamer and post

## What the child learns

Observation underpins many skills. For example, careful observation teaches children to pay attention to detail, a skill that is vital for early reading. Thinking about concepts such as more and less help with the skills that underpin mathematics.

It is impossible to see the wind but easy to see what it does. Mariners have a scale for the strength of the wind that uses the size and frequency of white horses on waves to judge how strong the wind is. If you live near the sea you can use a similar scale. If not, you could make your own scale by measuring how the wind moves certain plants in the garden. Devise the scale together and give it the child's name: the Jamie Scale for Wind, for example.

## what to do

Devise your scale, write it down, and pin it up on a bulletin board. A full Jamie Force Six would almost blow Jamie over, while a Jamie Force One does not even move the big stems of grass. In between, a Jamie Two occasionally moves the lightest leaves, a Jamie Three sets most leaves dancing, a Jamie Four moves whole plants, and a Jamie Five pushes soft plants over and shakes the branches of the trees.

The direction of the wind is best measured by feeling the wind on a damp finger. Lick the front of your finger and hold it up in the wind. It feels coldest when the full force of the wind is on the wet surface. But what direction is it? If you know which way your house faces, or where the sun sets, you can work this out and put in some markers. Better still, you can buy a small compass.

If you attach a small plastic streamer to a post, this will act like a wind sock to tell you which direction the wind is coming from. Put this in an exposed spot that will catch the wind in all directions.

# Windy day collage

When you get home from a windy walk it's time for a warming drink, a quiet chat, and a cuddle. Talking about outings stretches the child's vocabulary, and her memory. Making a collage is a quiet and calming activity that acts as a memory cue for the outing. It's a good activity for children to work on together, something to do when she has a friend around to play.

## what to do

On a large sheet of oak tag, build a picture of the child's outing. Spread glue on the surface of the collage for young children to place items onto; older children can apply the glue themselves.

Make the sky by putting cottonball clouds on a blue background.

Perhaps there is a kite made from paper or foil with a long string and a dangling tail. Attach one end of the tail and let the other hang free.

Raincoats can be made from bits of plastic, and a laundry line from string and bits of cloth.

Make a bonfire from bits of wooden lollipop sticks and toothpicks, red paper, and cottonball smoke.

Cut out pictures of small children and stick them in the picture.

Make the floor with fallen leaves and use yarn, sticks, and leaves to make bendy trees.

Details can be added with felt-tipped pens or crayons.

**CHECKLIST**

| | |
|---|---|
| age 2+ | |
| indoor | ✓ |
| no. of children | 1–2 children (working together or separately) |
| time | about 2–3 hours to make |
| help required | ✓ |
| messy | ✓ |

**EQUIPMENT**
- thick paper or oak tag
- glue and brushes
- pictures of small children
- collage materials: cottonballs, foil, string, plastic, sticks, cloth, lollipop sticks, toothpicks, yarn, leaves
- felt-tipped pens or crayons

## What the child learns

Lots of good hand–eye coordination skills, artistic expression, and good fine-finger control. Encourages self-confidence.

# Wind chimes

## CHECKLIST

age 4+ can make with help
age 2+ can enjoy

| | |
|---|---|
| indoor/outdoor | ✓ |
| no. of children | 1 |
| time | about 2 hours |
| help required | ✓ |
| messy | ✓ |

## EQUIPMENT

- 5 short sections of bamboo (of varying lengths and thickness, cut from garden canes)
- knitting needle or screwdriver
- drill with small bit
- sandpaper
- household paint and varnish
- string and large, blunt needle
- 1 cork coaster

## What the child learns

To help carry out a complicated activity. To follow instructions (vital for later schoolwork) and to be part of a communal activity (again something she will need to be able to do once she starts school).

Wind chimes make music as they catch the wind, but they also chime in a satisfying way when swiped by a small child as she passes. You can buy sets of chimes, but they are easy to make from hollowed-out bamboo canes—or you could do something more elaborate.

## what to do

Prepare the canes. Cut them into pieces of slightly different lengths, making the cut about 4 in. (10 cm) above a joint. Use a knitting needle or screwdriver to clear the pith from the middle of each one. Drill a small hole at an angle through the joint near the top of each cane. Four- to six-year-olds can do some of this under supervision, but you will need to do most of it for a younger child.

Rub the canes with sandpaper (even small children can help) and then paint them. Transfer a little household paint to a small container for the child. Or, instead of paint, she could use old nail polish. If the chimes are going to stay outside, weatherproof each cane by finishing with a coat of quick-drying varnish.

Arrange the bamboo canes in order of size with the holes roughly aligned. Poke the string through the hole at the top of the cane. This will be easier for the child to do if you make the hole at an angle and use a blunt needle to thread it through.

Keeping the string on the needle, push it through a coaster twice and tie it. Repeat this for each cane. Now push a string through the center of the coaster twice so that it forms a loop. Now tie the two sides of the loop together.

Place the wind chimes where they can catch the wind, and where the child can knock them either with a hand or with a stick as she passes. Just a gentle tap across the chimes will set them ringing.

Give the child a stopwatch and see if she can measure how long the sounds from a little tap, a gentle swipe, and a good whack take to die down.

# Parachutes

| indoor/outdoor | ✓ |
|---|---|
| no. of children | no limit |
| time | 10–15 minutes to make |
| help required | ✓ |
| no mess | ✓ |

**EQUIPMENT**

- squares of colored tissue paper or plastic
- lengths of thread, each 10 in. (25 cm) long
- adhesive tape
- modeling clay or adhesive gum
- scissors
- needle

## What the child learns

Hand–eye coordination is involved in making and launching the parachute. Simple scientific principles are demonstrated, and the child learns how the wind affects some forms.

**WARNING**
Make sure all activities involving an open upstairs window are supervised

**There is something rather magical about watching a parachute floating to earth, and a windy day adds an extra dimension!**

## what to do

### MAKING A PARACHUTE

Take a square of colored tissue paper or plastic (tissue paper works best, but most children find plastic easier to work with) and four lengths of thread. Tape a length of thread to each corner of the tissue paper or plastic sheet.

Bind the loose ends of the threads together with a lump of modeling clay or adhesive gum.

Have the child throw the parachute into the wind and watch it rise and fall.

You can drop the parachute from a height, such as an upstairs window, but you will need to hold the child tightly while she watches. Be sure the window is open only slightly. If you make two parachutes, you can compare what happens if you make a small hole in the center of one with a needle; this lets the air escape and the descent should be steadier.

The parachutes will not last long, but since they take such a short time to make you can start again the next time it is windy.

### OTHER ACTIVITIES

- In the spring, look for seed heads that can be thrown into the wind.

- In the fall, kick up the dead leaves on a windy day and see how many are caught by the wind.

# Wishing tree

In midsummer, Japanese children and their parents make wishes for the future. They write them on ribbons and hang them from the wishing tree. If your child has a summer birthday (or even if she does not) it's a nice activity for a sunny day. The tree can also be decorated with a few Christmas tree-style baubles.

## what to do

Give each child a felt-tipped pen and white ribbons, strips of white cotton from an old sheet, or parcel tags. Get them to write out their wishes for the year on them. Older children can do real writing; younger ones can draw pictures or scribble (it is a magic tree after all).

Choose a tree with branches low enough for a child to reach. Tie the ribbons on the branches of the tree where they can blow in the wind.

When all the ribbons are in place, play a game of *Here we go 'round the wishing tree* (to the tune of *Here we go 'round the mulberry bush*) while dancing around the tree and carrying out whatever actions each child chooses.

### Wishing tree song

*Here we go 'round the wishing tree, the wishing tree, the wishing tree.*
*Here we go 'round the wishing tree on a bright and windy morning.*
*This is the way we make a wish, make a wish, make a wish.*
*This is the way we make a wish on a bright and windy morning.*

**CHECKLIST**

| | |
|---|---|
| age 2+ | |
| outdoor | ✓ |
| no. of children | no limit |
| time | as long as you like |
| help required | ✓ |
| no mess | ✓ |

**EQUIPMENT**
- white ribbons, strips of white cotton from an old sheet, or package tags
- felt-tipped pens
- tree with low branches

## What the child learns

This is a simple activity and encourages children to play together. The child practices pen control and writing, thinks about the future, and enjoys the social occasion. It makes a good talking point.

# Blowing bubbles

| | |
|---|---|
| age 2+ | |
| indoor/outdoor | ✓ |
| no. of children | no limit |
| time | 5 minutes–1 hour |
| help required | to make bubble mix |
| messy | ✓ |

**EQUIPMENT**
- bubble solution
- old teapot and straws
- bubble bath
- bowls, wading pool (optional), and garden hose
- dish-washing liquid and bowl
- food coloring and paper
- bar of soap
- inner cardboard tube from a roll of paper towels or toilet paper
- absorbent material such as curtain tape
- sticks

## What the child learns
Confidence, pride in achievement. Breath control helps with singing and speech.

Bubbles are guaranteed to fill small children with glee. They love the way bubbles float, shine, and reflect colors; the way they stick together, change shape, and then, finally, burst.

## what to do
### GAMES WITH BUBBLES
Little jars of bubble solution with rings for blowing the bubbles are widely available. You can refill them with a mixture of dish-washing liquid and water. Let the children blow their own (although you may need to hold the jar).

Fill an old teapot with bubble solution, and use a straw to blow into the water via the spout. Watch the bubbles pile up around the rim.

At bath time, add bubble bath. Make bubble "gloves" or "socks" for the child. On a sunny day you could do this in the backyard.

Put dish-washing liquid or bubble bath into a bowl or wading pool and then fill with the hose on full force. The mound of bubbles can be used to make "swim suits" or to mold temporary "houses" with walls that soon pop and disappear.

### MAKING A BUBBLE PICTURE
Put water and dish-washing liquid into a bowl. Add a little food coloring and give children straws to blow a mass of bubbles.

Now place a sheet of paper (newspaper would do) on top of the bubbles. Lift off and set aside to dry, bubbles facing upward. The bubbles gradually pop, leaving a pattern of overlapping circles. This can make pretty wrapping paper.

## MAKING EXTRA BIG BUBBLES

Take a bowl of water, a bar of soap, and a tube—an empty toilet paper or paper towel roll would do, or just roll up a newspaper and stick it together with tape. Dip the end of the tube into the water, then rub it across the surface of the soap until there is a film of soap across the end—you may have to do it several times. Blow gently down the tube until you have a big bubble. With practice, enormous bubbles can be blown.

Another way to make big bubbles is to make a loop (about 10 in./25 cm diameter) from absorbent material such as curtain tape. Make two small loops in the tape, about a third of the circumference apart. Attach sticks to the tape by pushing them through the loops.

In a bowl, make up a solution of one measure of dish-washing liquid to five or six of water (you may need to experiment with this as the liquids vary in strength). Dip the entire loop into the liquid, holding the sticks together, and leave it to fully absorb the bubble solution. Then carefully lift out the loop and pull the sticks apart. You should get a big film across the loop. Move it gently against the breeze to make a truly giant bubble.

# Raindrop pictures

**CHECKLIST**

| | |
|---|---|
| age 2+ | |
| indoor/outdoor | ✓ |
| no. of children | no limit (it can get out of hand with a crowd!) |
| time | moments to prepare; 30 minutes to play |
| help required | to set up |
| messy | ✓ |

**EQUIPMENT**

- water containers
- paintbrushes
- food coloring (optional)
- surface to receive water droplets (paper, wall, window, for example)

## What the child learns

To understand cause and effect. To observe how water moves on a surface. The task is also good for hand–eye coordination. It can be great fun if more than one child is involved. Such glee helps to cement a small child's friendships and so helps the child develop social skills.

This is an indulgent game for the bathroom or kitchen or, better still, for the terrace or garden path. It's a subdued activity with a small paintbrush, extravagant with an emulsion brush, or just plain exuberant with a bucket of water, a group of kids, and the biggest brushes you can find.

## what to do

Select a surface to receive water flicks. A piece of paper, a plastic place mat, a tiled surface, the kitchen table, or, best of all, a large picture window. On a nice day it's easier, and less messy, to flick the water onto the outside of the window. A fence, pavement, or a wall could also be used to receive the water drops.

Provide each child with water and a brush. In the house these should be quite small; outside they can be bigger. You could also add food coloring to the water for more dramatic effects.

Dip the brush in the water, pull the wet bristles to one side using finger or thumb, and let go.

Alternatively, just shake the brush, or use a jerky over-arm movement to flick the water at the chosen surface.

# Little boats

**CHECKLIST**

| | |
|---|---|
| age 2+ | |
| indoor/outdoor | ✓ |
| no. of children | no limit |
| time | 30 minutes–half a day |
| help required | ✓ |
| messy | ✓ |

**EQUIPMENT**
- puddle or large bowl
- colored oak tag for the sails
- stickers and felt-tipped pens (optional)
- yogurt containers
- toothpicks or lollypop sticks for the masts
- scissors
- adhesive gum
- corks or small stones

Water is made for boats! Your child may have some toy boats of her own, but there is nothing like making your own and racing them with a friend. If it's too wet to go out, their boats can make their maiden voyage in a large bowl filled with water.

## what to do

Cut out a sail from the oak tag (decorate with stickers or draw on a design if you wish).

Pierce the sail at the top and bottom and thread the mast through the holes.

Attach the mast to the inside of the yogurt container with some adhesive gum, then weight the bottom of the boat with corks or small stones. Her boat is now ready to make its maiden voyage!

## What the child learns

To play with something she has made herself. Good for hand–eye coordination. Teaches her about materials that sink and float.

# Making a rain gauge

**CHECKLIST**

| | |
|---|---|
| age 4+ | |
| indoor/outdoor | ✓ |
| no. of children | 1–3 |
| time | 30 minutes to half a day |
| help required | ✓ |
| messy | ✓ |

**EQUIPMENT**

- rain
- large roasting pan
- turkey baster
- stickers and felt-tipped pens (optional)
- funnel
- measuring cup or baby's feeding bottle
- paper and pens

## What the child learns

Measuring, recording, and keeping records are the perfect training for a young scientist. Careful observation teaches children to pay attention to detail and is excellent for developing early reading. Counting and comparing numbers play a part in this activity, too.

It may seem like a downpour but unless the rain is constant there may not be enough to measure. Meteorologists make accurate rain measurements by collecting rain in a wide container and pouring it into a narrow tube, which magnifies the depth.

## what to do

Collect the rain in a large roasting pan.

Suck up the rain from the pan with a turkey baster and transfer to a measuring cup or baby's feeding bottle—use a funnel if you have one.

Record the amount of rain in a book or on a weather chart (see page 116).

Is there more rain in the morning than in the afternoon? Which is the wettest day since the child's records began?

# Watching raindrops

On a wet day when children are stuck in the house, why not watch the raindrops on the windowpane? How will this one move? Will it go straight or zigzag across the pane? Will it reach the bottom or stop halfway? It's a good betting game (if you approve), which can also help children to count and do simple addition.

## what to do

Watch individual raindrops as they slide down the window.

Pick two and see which travels the furthest, reaches the lowest point, or gets swallowed up the soonest.

If children are betting on the result, they should pick their raindrops and place their bets—winner takes all. At the end of each turn, count out the new totals. One from you and two from me, that makes one, two, three!

Look at how raindrops behave on different windows around the house. How do raindrops behave when the rain is lashing against the window? How do they behave when the rain is falling straight down?

**CHECKLIST**

| age 3+ | |
| --- | --- |
| indoor | ✓ |
| no. of children | 1–2 |
| time | 10–30 minutes |
| no help required | ✓ |
| no mess | ✓ |

**EQUIPMENT**
- window the child can sit or stand beside
- rain
- buttons or tokens for betting

## What the child learns

Simple observation, looking for detail, predicting patterns and, if you bet, simple counting and arithmetic.

# Making a weather chart

age 2–4+

| | |
|---|---|
| indoor/outdoor | ✓ |
| no. of children | 1–2 |
| time | 1 hour to make chart, 10 minutes– 1 hour each day to make records |
| help required | ✓ |
| messy | ✓ |

**EQUIPMENT**

- oak tag, ruler, pen, and adhesive gum for chart
- symbols drawn or printed onto adhesive paper
- outdoor thermometer with large figures
- rain gauge (see page 114)

## What the child learns

Observational skills. Counting. Measuring. Recording and keeping records. Making decisions (something that is often difficult for a small child). Learning about an ordered sequence: a little rain, more rain, and lots of rain, for example.

Come rain or shine, your child can be a weather girl. She may not be able to tell you what the weather will be like tomorrow, but she can record what she sees and she can make predictions and see if they come true!

## what to do

### MAKING A WEATHER CHART

For a young child (two to three years old), a chart covering a week is probably long enough, but an older child (four or more) may enjoy keeping records for a month at a time. Decide what you are going to record on each day.

To make the chart, take a sheet of oak tag and draw boxes for each day, making sure the space is big enough for all the information the child wants to record. Write the day and date at the top of each square. After you have drawn the boxes, she can draw some decorations around the border.

Fix the chart to a wall at a height she can easily reach. An ongoing activity such as this needs to be on view if it is to sustain the child's interest.

### RECORDING TEMPERATURE AND RAIN

Taking and recording the temperature is rather difficult for a two- to three-year-old, but by four a child can do this with help.

Look in garden centers and toy shops for a thermometer with large figures that can stay outside. A bright six-year-old may like a maximum/minimum thermometer, especially if she likes to collect facts and figures.

If you have made a rain gauge (see page 114), she can record rainfall, too. Enter the readings onto the chart or get her to do it if she is old enough.

# Making the symbols

The simplest way to keep weather records is to use symbols. You will need different ones for sun, wind, rain, fog, in the winter, snow and frost as well. You could use your computer to generate symbols and print these on address labels or get her to draw simple pictures on sheets of colored adhesive paper: Use blue for rain, yellow for sun, white for snow, black for clouds, and so on.

The child can then stick the appropriate symbols on each day. Or if each block features every symbol, then check them or put stickers against them. Decide how you are going to record how windy or sunny it is. For example, you could use a half sun to record that the day was not very sunny.

# Rainbows

| | |
|---|---|
| age 2–6 | |
| indoor/outdoor | ✓ |
| no. of children | no limit |
| time | 30 minutes–1 hour |
| help required | ✓ |
| messy | ✓ |

**EQUIPMENT**

- felt-tipped pens or crayons
- paper
- hose with a spray nozzle
- a sunny day!
- cups of water and red, yellow, and deep blue paint; a paintbrush for each pot
- coffee filters (or blotting paper) and holder in a cup, water-soluble ink, food coloring or water-soluble markers in red, yellow, and blue for cones
- eye-dropper, stiff brush, and cocktail stick
- paper towels, apron, wipes, and floor covering to control mess

## What the child learns

How to mix colors, and what happens when certain colors mix. Careful observation is encouraged, as is good pen and brush control and artistic expression. These activities are excellent for hand–eye coordination.

A rainbow can be seen only when the sun shines through falling raindrops, which then reflect back the colors of the spectrum. The rainbow is always seen on the side opposite the sun. Younger as well as older children enjoy creating their own rainbows. Make sure the child (and immediate surroundings) is well covered because even water-soluble colors can be difficult to remove.

## what to do

**MAKE YOUR OWN RAINBOWS**

Draw a rainbow. The order of the colors is red (outside), orange, yellow, green, blue, indigo (a deep blue), and violet (inside).

When the sun is shining, stand with your child so that you have your backs to the sun and make a fine mist with a hose. With luck, you should see mini-rainbows.

Take a sheet of absorbent paper, a cup of water, and cups of red, yellow, and dark blue paint.

Moisten the paper all over by painting it with clear water. Now show the child how to make arcs of color starting with red, then yellow, and then blue, leaving a small space between the colors for them to blend together to make all the colors of the rainbow.

## MAKING COLOR CONES

Place a coffee filter (or some blotting paper) into a holder and rest it on a cup. Dampen the filter by pouring a little water through it. Have ready three bottles of water-soluble ink or food coloring in red, yellow, and blue.

Put a few drops of each color onto the filter (the easiest way to do this is with an eye-dropper). The three colors should be fairly close together so that when they spread across the wet paper they will mix.

Encourage the child to watch what happens where the colors meet. At the intersection of red and yellow you get orange; of blue and yellow, green; of blue and red, purple. Where all three colors mix, you will get brown and black.

For a messier activity, spray the color onto wet blotting paper by dipping a small stiff brush into the ink, bending back the bristles with a finger or cocktail stick, taking aim at the paper, and letting go.

To keep mess to a minimum, get the child to draw a rainbow on the dry filters using water-soluble markers. Then dribble water onto the filters with an eye-dropper. This approach is more suitable for a younger child.

Less messy still: Rest water-soluble markers against the wet filter and let the color flow out of the pens onto the paper.

When the child has made his filters, allow them to dry and thread them on knotted string to make a rainbow mobile to hang up.

# A walk in the rain

**CHECKLIST**

| | |
|---|---|
| age 2+ | |
| outdoor | ✓ |
| no. of children | no limit |
| time | 1–2 hours |
| help required | supervision |
| messy | wet |

**EQUIPMENT**

- rain
- raincoats, boots, and umbrellas

### What the child learns
Observational skills. Opportunities for later story telling and for remembering what she did.

On yet another wet afternoon, when the children are fed up and unruly, why not abandon the drawing and painting and meet the weather head-on? Most children do not mind being out in the rain as long as they are properly dressed for it.

## what to do

Search for puddles. Jump over them, splash in them, stir them up with sticks, and watch how the water moves.

Throw a few leaves, bits of wood, or twigs into the puddle and then jump again. What happens?

Find a muddy bit of ground and let the child watch the mud ooze around her waterproof boots.

Watch the raindrops fall in the puddle, pond, or lake. Look at the ripples. Throw in some stones and see how much bigger the ripples are now.

What do ducks do in the rain? Take some seed to feed them: They will be ready for it, especially if all the other children have stayed home.

Look up at the sky. What do rain clouds look like? Can the child see the difference between the sky when it is raining and when it is just dull? Talk about different sorts of skies.

Look at the water drops on the plants and look for worms that have come up to the surface. What has happened to all the other animals?

In town, look for places where cars will send up a spray of water. Watch what happens when cars drive through puddles. Watch the water rushing away into the drains. See lights reflected in the water and people rushing from place to place huddled under umbrellas.

Then go home (or out) for a nice warm drink and to talk about all you have seen.

# A big happy sun picture

Children love to draw the sun. It's one of the first things that we can recognize in their pictures, and one of the first things they draw in a representative way—after all, the sun does not really have all those ray lines that children draw.

## what to do

Get the child to draw a simple sun picture; he needs paper, felt-tipped pens, or red and yellow paint.

You can make a more elaborate collage by drawing a big circle on a sheet of paper (use a plate as a template); then carefully spread glue inside the circle. Carefully drop orange lentils onto the glue. Let this dry and shake off the excess. To make the sunshine, add a few sequins.

To make rays from the edge of the sun, draw lines, stick on sequins, or soak some toothpicks in a mixture of red and yellow food coloring, and stick them on.

You could fill the sun with bits of orange, red, and yellow cloth and make the rays out of yarn.

For a really elaborate picture, cut out a skyline in black paper and make the setting sun from coiled-up yarn.

**CHECKLIST**

| | |
|---|---|
| age 3+ | |
| indoor | ✓ |
| no. of children | 1 |
| time | 1 hour to half a day |
| help required | ✓ |
| messy | ✓ |

**EQUIPMENT**

- paper or card
- felt-tipped pens or red and yellow paint
- plate
- glue
- orange lentils, sequins, and toothpicks
- red and yellow food coloring
- orange, red, and yellow fabric scraps and yarn (optional)
- scissors
- black paper

## What the child learns

To work toward an end and the self-confidence of having achieved something. To express himself artistically. Good pen control and good hand–eye coordination.

# Making a sundial

Is it lunchtime? The child's tummy will tell him, of course, but on a sunny day you can verify the fact by reading a simple sundial.

## what to do

Select a spot that gets the sun all day, and put a marker where the child will stand.

The child will need to stand on this spot three times during the day to set up the clock: at breakfast time, at lunchtime, and at snack time.

Mark the position of his shadow each time he stands on the designated spot. You could use pebbles, flower pots, or sidewalk chalk. Call the markers by the name of the meal.

Next time you need to check if it is lunchtime, get him to stand on the spot and see where his shadow falls in relation to the lunchtime marker.

**CHECKLIST**

| age 2+ | |
| --- | --- |
| outdoor | ✓ |
| no. of children | 1 |
| time | 1 hour to prepare, moments to check the time |
| help required | ✓ |
| no mess | ✓ |

**EQUIPMENT**
- a sunny spot
- chalk, flower pots, or pebbles to use as markers

## What the child learns

This is very simple science and an opportunity to ask questions. Why does the position of the shadow move? Why is it the same each day? It's an activity the child can come back to weeks later, and remember the day he made it.

# Sunshine and shadows

**CHECKLIST**

| | |
|---|---|
| age 3+ | |
| indoor/outdoor | ✓ |
| no. of children | no limit |
| time | from a few minutes to a few hours! |
| help required | ✓ |
| no mess | ✓ |

**EQUIPMENT**

- sun
- moon
- streetlights
- flashlight
- rope

## What the child learns

This is simple science at its best. It allows the child to make simple experiments, to ask "what if I...," and to find the answer. It is excellent training in simple observational skills and gives the child the confidence to know that he can find out what happens if he tries.

Children are fascinated by shadows. They love the way their shadows follow them around. When the sun is high, the shadows are short; at the end of the day, the shadows are much longer. At night there are shadows from the streetlights and sometimes from the moon, as well.

## what to do

On a sunny day let him dance around and watch how his shadow dances with him.

Get him to stand beside still water with the sun behind him. Where is his shadow now? He may lose his shadow because the water surface is too dark and reflective to pick out the shadow easily, but he will get a reflection instead.

At what time of day is his shadow just as long as he is? Use a length of rope to measure how tall he is. At various times of the day he can check this against his shadow. The time he is just as long as his shadow will be different for different children, and will change as the sun gets higher or lower in the sky in the different seasons. You could keep a record of this time.

Take a walk down the street at night and watch the shadows grow longer and shorter between the lights. Sometimes he has two shadows, sometimes even more. Find out what is causing the shadows and watch how each of them changes.

On a clear moonlit night go out into the background and find your moon shadows. You could do a little dance or pretend to be dogs howling at the moon.

Shine a flashlight directly behind the child to make a really big shadow. Let him stand in front of a wall. When does the head of his shadow disappear over the top? (You may need to shine the flashlight from a low position to get a really long shadow.)

Can you make animal shadows on the wall? The simplest one is a dog's head: Make your hand flat, turn it sideways, parallel with the wall, stick up your thumb for the dog's ear, and move your little finger down to open the dog's mouth.

A bird is easy to make, too. Hook your thumbs together and spread your fingers to make wings; then flap them as you lift your arms up and down.

To make a fox, bend your middle two fingers down to meet your thumb. This forms the snout. Keep your index and little finger straight up in the air to make the fox's ears.

# Snowstorm

**EQUIPMENT**

- plastic bottles or jars or small glass jars
- detergent
- food coloring
- water
- coconut or oatmeal
- holiday cake decorations
- leaves and foil (optional)
- glitter
- glue
- glycerine (from a pharmacy)

## What the child learns

This is a very simple but enjoyable activity that will amuse a small child for a few minutes. There is a real sense of achievement when a child manages to make something for himself. Small babies love the glitter version; it would be a nice toy for an older sibling to make.

There is something magical about shaking up a bottle and watching the "snow" settle. The best shakers are made from clear jars and glitter, but you can make a simple shaker from a clear plastic bottle and a little oatmeal or coconut. It will get cloudy after a while, but you can always make another.

## what to do

To amuse a small child for a few minutes, half-fill a clear plastic bottle or jar with water, add a few drops of detergent and a little food coloring. Give the bottle a vigorous shake and let him watch the bubbles subside.

For a quick and simple snow scene, put some water in a clear bottle or jar and add coconut or oatmeal. For a sea scene, add a few leaves and some small, silver foil fish.

For a really special snow scene, stick holiday cake decorations to the inside of the lid of a wide-necked jar. Fill with glycerine and add some glitter. Seal, shake, and enjoy the snowstorm.

# Making a snow scene

This is a three-dimensional picture created on a tray. It makes a pleasant change from painting and collage work.

## what to do

A tray makes a good base because it keeps everything in place, but a small table or a large sheet of stiff oak tag would work.

Although cotton is the obvious material to use for snow, it does not offer much support for the things the child might want to stand on it. A better base is one made from a sheet of white oak tag with a light coating of confectioner's sugar and some little puffs of cotton flecked with glitter.

Lay out an everyday scene with roads, lawns, houses, cars, animals, and people. Use holiday decorations, plastic animals and people, play dough models, cars—whatever is appropriate from the toy chest.

Make a frozen pond with a mirror. Dust it with a little confectioner's sugar and throw some pine needles on the surface.

**CHECKLIST**

| | |
|---|---|
| age 3+ | |
| indoor | ✓ |
| no. of children | no limit |
| time | about 1 hour |
| help required | ✓ |
| messy | ✓ |

**EQUIPMENT**
- small tray, table, or stiff piece of white oak tag
- confectioner's sugar, cotton, and glitter for the snow
- holiday cake and tree decorations, plastic animals and people, play dough models, cars for the scene
- mirror and pine needles for the pond

## What the child learns

This is a variation on the usual collage—not as long lasting but good for the younger child who cannot yet draw. It gives a very realistic picture, which gives children a sense of achievement. It's a task that works toward an end, and uses hand–eye coordination and artistic expression.

# A snowy day

**CHECKLIST**

| | |
|---|---|
| age 2+ | |
| outdoor | ✓ |
| no. of children | no limit |
| time | 1 hour (or until the children start to get cold) |
| help required | ✓ |
| messy | ✓ |

**EQUIPMENT**

- snow
- warm clothes and waterproof gloves for the children
- carrot, pebbles, scarf, and hat for the snowman
- blunt knife
- magnifying glass
- containers for ice
- bird food

## What the child learns

To look at the world in a different way. To make an instant impression. To build, to have fun. Because most children are excited by the first snow, it's very easy to make friends.

Waking up to the first snow of the year is always exciting. Even before the curtains are opened to reveal all, there is often a quality of light and sound that tells you that the snow is there.

## what to do

### MAKE YOUR MARK

Encourage your child to make fresh footprints in virgin snow and fall over (if he is dressed for it), making an imprint of his body in the snow.

Create a mystery for those who come along next by showing him how to walk out into the virgin snow and then carefully walk backward in his own footprints.

Show him how to make snowballs and throw them at a wall or a tree. Enjoy the splat!

Start with a small snowball and roll it along the ground so it picks up more snow and gets bigger and bigger and bigger.

Roll the big snowball, leaving a wide trail. Make the trail more interesting by writing "We were here first" in the snow or drawing a big stick man and a small fat dog. You could write or draw with footprints, too.

Build a snowman. Two big snowballs, one on top of the other, are a good starting point. You can then show him how to pack the snow around the neck and the base. A simple snowman just needs a carrot nose, some pebble eyes, a hat, and a scarf and he is finished.

If he wants to elaborate, you can show him how to use the snow as a basis to make a rabbit, tortoise, fish, or whatever takes his fancy! Snow castles, snow teddies, snow dogs, and even snow houses are possible if you have a blunt knife to cut the snow to shape for him. It's a good medium to work in, since it cuts easily and, if you make a mistake, you can just put on a new bit of snow and start again.

## SNOW STUDIES

When it is very cold, snowflakes are larger and more distinctly patterned. Look through a magnifying glass to study the flakes that have fallen on his coat.

On a cold night, put out several containers of different shapes. In the morning, collect the ice that will have formed in them. With luck, you may be able to get a whole sheet out at a time.

Go to the pond and watch the ducks trying to land.

This weather is hard work for birds, so give them some bird seed and nuts. See page 95 for how to make a bird pudding.

Look for icicles; carry them home and watch them melt.

arts

and crafts

# Get ready to paint

CHECKLIST

age 2–6

| | |
|---|---|
| indoor | ✓ |
| no. of children | no limit |
| time | 10 minutes to half a day |
| help required | to start |
| messy | ✓ |

**EQUIPMENT**
- paper
- powder paint and paint jars
- soap flakes or flour to thicken paint
- food coloring (optional)
- paintbrushes
- jars of water to wash brushes
- paper towels, apron, wipes, and floor covering to control mess

## What the child learns
Painting and drawing activities teach children that they can make things happen. They learn pen control, and to express themselves artistically. They feel proud of their achievement.

Painting and drawing are very satisfying for a small child. She dips in the brush and puts it on the paper and the effect is instant. Not only can she see the effect her action has had, she can change what she has done by taking a second dip into the paint jar. Most children need little encouragement.

## what to do

### CHOOSING AND MAKING PAINT
Small children find watercolors much too difficult. They add far too much water to the block and end up with a messy paint box; and if they put too much water on the paper, everything runs.

Powder paints are far better for small children than ready-made paint, especially if they are

thickened with soap flakes or flour. Add the soap flakes (not detergent) to the paint after it is mixed, and stir well until it dissolves.

To thicken with flour, put a tablespoon of flour into a saucepan with a little water and whisk it. Heat gently and keep stirring until it thickens. Stir in food coloring or powder paint and mix well.

Two- to three-year-olds need only one color. For older children, make up 2–4 jars of color and use a separate brush for each one. You can buy no-spill paint jars from art suppliers and good toy stores, and these are well worth seeking out.

## CHOOSING PAPER
Fairly thick absorbent paper is the best surface for powder paint. You can buy it at good toy stores and art suppliers, but recycled paper is fine, too. You can use up old computer printouts, letters, and even the back of wallpaper samples (coated wallpaper is less likely to rip when wet).

## CHOOSING YOUR MEDIUM
Short-handled paintbrushes are easiest for small hands. Choose ones with larger heads for younger children; fine brushes require fine-finger control. As children grow up, introduce finer brushes that allow them to achieve more detail in their paintings.

The same rule applies to crayons. Start with short stubby crayons, and once the child has finer finger control, introduce her to longer and thinner crayons.

Felt-tipped pens are great for young children, but restrict the number available at any one time. Children are much more likely to leave the caps off if they have too many colors in use at one time. Offer the child the box and let her choose five or six. Always check that they are water soluble, and if you find that certain colors do not come out in the wash, ban them!

# Ink blots

CHECKLIST

| | |
|---|---|
| age 2–6 | |
| indoor | ✓ |
| no. of children | no limit |
| time | 30 minutes–2 hours |
| help required | to fold the paper |
| messy | ✓ |

**EQUIPMENT**

- paper (not too absorbent or thin)
- thickened paint (see pages 132–133)
- paintbrush
- paper towels, apron, wipes, and floor covering to control mess

## What the child learns

This activity encourages artistic expression and teaches children that they can make things happen. To feel pride and confidence through a sense of achievement.

On most days, children are perfectly happy with a jar of paint, a brush, and a piece of paper. But if they are a bit out of sorts, or if they feel in an "I can't" mood, this is an activity that gives pleasing results for a minimum of effort. It is also an excellent way for a child who feels he is clumsy and relatively unskilled to create a pleasing picture and thus to make him feel proud of his artistic achievement.

## what to do

Take a sheet of paper and fold it down the middle. Lay it on the table and open it like a book. The child now drops a blob of thickened paint onto the paper, refolds the paper, and smoothes it, thus spreading the thickened paint. Open it up and see what he has made.

Two dollops of paint give even more interesting results. Choose contrasting colors that mix, such as red and yellow, black and white, or blue and yellow.

Four- to six-year-olds can use this technique to make a warm tonal painting in reds and yellows or a cool painting in blues and greens. Use a fairly wide brush to draw lines of colors on one side of the fold. Continue some of these across the fold. Fold the sheet as above and then open out. Use the paint to fill in spaces and fold again.

# Drops

This is another simple activity that works well with younger children. Be warned, though, it could get rather messy, especially if a group of children are painting together! Have plenty of wipes and paper towels on hand to clean up.

## what to do

This activity looks at how paint rolls after it has been dropped. The ideal surface to use is a piece of shiny, but still absorbent, oak tag. The idea is that the paint should remain on top of the paper long enough for it to move, but it should then sink in before the next drop is applied.

The best paint to use is one that has been slightly thickened so that it still flows easily but not too fast. An older child might enjoy experimenting with different surfaces and thicknesses of paint.

Use a fine brush to drop a small blob of paint on the surface. Lift the oak tag and tip it so the paint runs down, then tip it back to move the stream of paint in another direction.

Drop half-a-dozen large blobs of paint onto a plate and tip the plate from side to side to create a pattern. You could use a paper plate and make a print of the result for posterity.

**CHECKLIST**

| | |
|---|---|
| age 3–6 | |
| indoor | ✓ |
| no. of children | no limit |
| time | 30 minutes–2 hours |
| help required | to start |
| messy | ✓ |

**EQUIPMENT**
- sheets of fairly shiny, absorbent oak tag
- thickened paint (see pages 132–133)
- fine paintbrush
- plate and paper plates
- paper towels, apron, wipes, and floor covering to control mess

## What the child learns
Reinforces the message that children can make things happen. This is another way of producing a pleasing effect without a great deal of skill.

# Blow painting

Younger children will love this activity, as will older children who feel like doing something different. It is very messy, so have plenty of baby wipes to clean up their hands, and paper towels to clean up any spills.

## CHECKLIST

| | |
|---|---|
| age 3–6 | |
| indoor | ✓ |
| no. of children | no limit |
| time | 30 minutes–1 hour |
| help required | to start |
| messy | ✓ |

## EQUIPMENT

- powder paint (not thickened)
- paper (not too thin)
- straws
- tray lined with foil
- paper towels, apron, wipes, and floor covering to control mess

## What the child learns

Artistic expression and learning "I can." Breath control and seeing what happens next.

## what to do

Make up some paint, but do not thicken it. Select a piece of paper—not too absorbent, because the child needs the paint to remain on the surface long enough for him to blow it around.

Drop a blob of paint on the paper and blow it to make the paint move over the surface of the paper in different directions.

An older child could blow down a straw, but supervise him and make sure the straw does not come into contact with the paint, as children sometimes suck the paint up into the straw.

Try putting half a dozen large blobs of thin paint onto a tray that is lined with foil, then blow these around with a straw until satisfied with the result. Make prints to keep by pressing paper down carefully onto the paint.

# Sprinkle, sprinkle

This is another activity that works well with younger children or with older children who want to try something new. It gives very similar results to flicking paint but is not nearly as messy, and it is a good way to achieve impressive results quite easily.

## what to do

You will need paint that has not been thickened, a sheet of fairly absorbent paper, a stiff bristle brush, and a fine-mesh tea strainer.

Dip the bristle brush into the paint. Holding the strainer over the paper, push and work the brush against the mesh to produce a fine rain of paint drops. Move the strainer around so these are spread over the paper. Work with one color at a time, cleaning the brush and the strainer between colors.

If you have one, a potato ricer could be used to make bigger spots. Instead of a brush, soak a sponge in colored paint and put it into the ricer, then gently squeeze the handle.

| CHECKLIST | |
| --- | --- |
| age 4–6 | |
| indoor | ✓ |
| no. of children | no limit |
| time | 30 minutes–2 hours |
| help required | to start |
| messy | ✓ |

### EQUIPMENT

- powder paint (not thickened)
- absorbent paper
- stiff bristle brush
- fine-mesh strainer
- potato ricer and sponge (optional)
- paper towels, apron, wipes, and floor covering to control mess

## What the child learns

To express himself artistically. That he can make things happen. If a child is aware he is relatively unskilled, this is an excellent way for him to make a pleasing picture.

# Finger and hand painting

**CHECKLIST**

| | |
|---|---|
| age 2–6 | |
| indoor/outdoor | ✓ |
| no. of children | no limit |
| time | 30 minutes–2 hours |
| help required | ✓ |
| messy | ✓ |

**EQUIPMENT**

- thickened paint
  (see page 132–133)
- absorbent paper or
  plastic surface
- cup
- baking tray or wide dish
- plastic tray
- bowl
- roll of wallpaper
- newspaper
- paper towels, apron, wipes, and
  floor covering to control mess

## What the child learns

Painting and drawing activities
give artistic expression and
teach children that they can
make things happen. They
are excellent for hand–eye
coordination and can also
be lots of fun.

This activity works well with younger and
older children alike. Beware, it is *very* messy
so have plenty of cleaning materials on
hand. Remember that the first print you
make is always poor, so use a piece of old
newspaper for each first new print.

## what to do

### FINGER AND HAND PAINTING

Make up some thickened paint and put it into
a cup. The child simply dips one or more of her
fingers into the paint and uses them to draw on
a sheet of paper or a plastic surface.

Make up some thickened paint—one color is
enough—and pour it into a wide dish or baking

tray. Show her how to use the flat and sides of her hand and her fingers to make different patterns.

Show her how to use the side of her fist to make the center of a sunflower and the side of her hand to make the petals.

For a really messy game, pour little pools of thickened paint onto a plastic tray. Then let her use her hands to arrange these into a pattern. Prints can then be taken of the result; discard the first one, which is not usually very good.

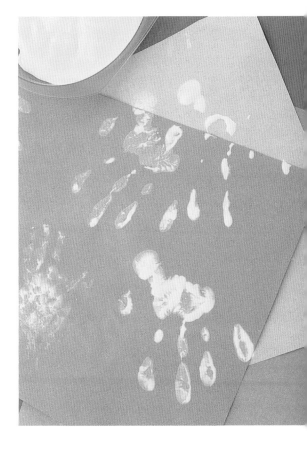

## FOOTPRINTS

Put some thickened paint in a bowl and take it out into the yard. Sweep the terrace or garden path and roll out a large length of wallpaper, print side down. Weigh down the edges.

Let the child step into the paint and then onto the paper.

A less messy version of this activity can be carried out with a bowl of water and dry paving slabs.

# Painting with sponges

**CHECKLIST**

| | |
|---|---|
| age 3–6 | |
| indoor | ✓ |
| no. of children | no limit |
| time | 30 minutes–2 hours |
| help required | to start |
| messy | ✓ |

**EQUIPMENT**

- powder paint
- dishes
- paper
- oak tag for templates
- pencil
- scissors or knife
- sponges or sheet of foam, 2–4 in. (5–10 cm) thick
- foam paint roller (optional)
- paper towels, apron, wipes, and floor covering to control mess

## What the child learns

Good for hand–eye coordination, hand skills, and learning to see a task through to a desired end. A great confidence builder, too.

It is much easier for a small child to use a sponge than a brush. Older children can use sponges to produce a solid block of color in a painting, and by placing the sponge directly down onto the surface of the paper it's possible to get rather delicate blocks of color that are broken up with little holes. This technique is ideal for painting the sky.

## what to do

### PAINTING

Make up paint in various colors in dishes. Thin paint will give a more even finish, while thickened paint shows off the texture.

Dip the sponge into the paint and then, depending on the finish wanted, either wipe it across the surface of the paper to give an even block of color, or place the sponge firmly on the paper for a textured finish. Dabbing it gives a result somewhere between the two.

## MAKING FOAM TEMPLATES

Decide on the shapes you want; these could be simple, like squares and circles, or more complex, like rabbits, cats, or leaves. Using pictures or real objects around which you have drawn as a guide, draw the desired shapes on a piece of oak tag and cut around them to make a template.

Take a sheet of foam, about 2–4 in. (5–10 cm) thick, and cut out the shapes using the oak tag templates.

## USING FOAM TEMPLATES

The child dips the foam into a dish of paint and carefully places it onto a sheet of oak tag or paper to make a picture.

Pictures can be built up from parts, such as the tops of trees, which are dipped into green paint, and the trunk of the tree, which is dipped into brown.

Wrapping paper can be made by repeatedly stamping the shapes onto paper.

Try cutting a pattern into an inexpensive foam paint roller.

# Painting with rags

CHECKLIST

| | |
|---|---|
| age 3–6 | |
| indoor | ✓ |
| no. of children | no limit |
| time | 30 minutes–2 hours |
| help required | to start |
| messy | ✓ |

**EQUIPMENT**

- thickened paint
  (see pages 132–133)
- saucers
- rags (natural fibers: old cotton
  sheets, chamois leather)
- rubber bands
- paper
- paint roller or rolling pin
- baking tray
- yarn
- paper towels, apron, wipes and
  floor covering to control mess

## What the child learns

Good for hand–eye
coordination, hand skills, and
learning to see a task through
to a desired end. A great
confidence builder, too.

**Rags are easier for a small child to paint
with than a paintbrush. A piece of
scrunched-up rag dipped into a dish of
paint can create some interesting patterns.**

## what to do

RAG PAINTING

Make up some fairly thick paint and put it into
a saucer. The child can use more than one color,
but each one will need a separate rag.

The rags need to be absorbent, so use natural
fibers. Roll up the rag: Aim for a loose roll with
interesting edges and folds rather than
something smooth and uniform. Tie in knots
and/or keep in place with rubber bands.

Get the child to dip the rag into the paint and
wipe, dab, or lightly place it onto the paper.

# Rolling

Wrap yarn around a small paint roller, then coat with paint and make some interesting patterns.

Before you attach the rags, paint a single-color wash using a paint roller and dilute paint. Then attach the rags and paint over the top with slightly thicker paint that is a few shades lighter or darker than the wash pattern surface.

## RAG ROLLING

Rag rolling is another technique that an older child can use to achieve an interesting all-over pattern—ideal for making wrapping paper.

Roughly cover a small rolling pin or a paint roller with a piece of old sheet or an old chamois leather—the surface of the cloth should have interesting folds and bumps. Secure the ends with rubber bands so that it looks like a firecracker.

Pour some thickened paint onto a baking tray and roll the pin or roller in the tray to coat the rag with paint.

Show the child how to make one roll on some scrap paper to take off excess paint, then roll it over the surface of her own paper.

# Templates and stencils

**CHECKLIST**

| | |
|---|---|
| age 3–6 | |
| indoor | ✓ |
| no. of children | no limit |
| time | 30 minutes–2 hours |
| help required | to start |
| messy | ✓ |

**EQUIPMENT**

- templates and stencils
- oak tag, pencil, scissors (to make your own template)
- paper
- paint
- brushes (including a stencil brush and an old toothbrush)
- sponge
- cocktail stick
- glue
- lentils
- crayons or soft pencil (4B)
- adhesive tape or adhesive gum
- paper towels, apron, wipes, and floor covering to control mess

## What the child learns

Good for hand–eye coordination, hand skills, and learning to see a task through to a desired end. Templates and stencils make very attractive pictures, and this gives the child a lot of confidence.

Bought stencils are easy to use and make very attractive pictures. Your own templates are simple to make and just as easy to use. Give the child a big brush, a sponge, or a rag and show him how to paint around the template or dab the spaces in his stencil.

## what to do

### MAKING TEMPLATES AND STENCILS

You can use real objects such as plates, a pair of scissors, or leaves as templates. Or you could cut out pictures from magazines and use those instead.

Alternatively, make your own stencils from paper or oak tag by drawing around objects and cutting out the shapes.

To make a simple stencil, fold a piece of paper into four and snip off the corners. Unfold to reveal a stencil with a symmetrical pattern.

### USING TEMPLATES AND STENCILS

Put the template on the paper and paint around it.

Put the stencil on the paper and paint through the holes using a stencil brush or a sponge.

Put your keys on the paper, dip an old toothbrush in the paint, and show the child how to bend the bristles to spray the paint onto the paper around the keys.

Load a toothbrush with paint, place it in the middle of the paper, and use a cocktail stick to bend the bristles. The brush acts as a template and the mess is reduced. (The child will need to hold the toothbrush steady.)

Put a template on the paper. Sponge, flick, or drip paint all over the surface, including the template. When the paint is dry, carefully lift off the template. The child can then paint the inner section with a contrasting color.

Spread glue around the template and drop lentils on it. Lift off the template and carefully paint the middle section.

# Making a rubbing

Find objects with texture to take the rubbings from, such as coins, leaves, or a textured pavement, for example. The child will need a crayon or a very soft pencil with which to make the rubbings.

Fix the paper in place using adhesive tape or adhesive gum. Carefully rub the pencil or crayon back and forth over the surface until a picture of the object appears. Do not press too hard.

# Waxworks

CHECKLIST

age 4–6

| | |
|---|---|
| indoor | ✓ |
| no. of children | no limit |
| time | 30 minutes–2 hours |
| help required | ✓ |
| messy | ✓ |

EQUIPMENT
- powder paint, food coloring
- paper
- wax candles, wax crayons
- paintbrush or pieces of sponge for spreading wash
- cardboard
- chopsticks or cocktail sticks
- paper towels, apron, wipes, and floor covering to control mess

## What the child learns

Like all artistic activities, making wax pictures teaches children that they can make things happen, improves their fine-finger control and hand–eye coordination, and allows them to express themselves artistically. Such a "magic" activity allows them to experiment.

Wax paintings always have an element of magic that delights children. The techniques all have two stages, which children over four will be able to manage.

## what to do

### WAX AND WASH

Make a color wash from a little powder paint dissolved in water or a little food coloring in water. Check to see that there is enough color in the mixture to make a transparent wash of color by painting a test piece on scrap paper.

Draw a small design on a sheet of paper with a clear wax candle, then cover with the color wash. After the paper has dried, repeat the process, extending the original drawing or drawing in a different place. Repeated washes gradually increases the depth of color, but wax fixes an area so the color does not get any deeper with subsequent washes over that area.

### CRAYON AND PAINT

Draw a picture using wax crayons, then wash over the picture with a color wash (see above) or with thickened powder paints. The paint does not stick to the crayon and so the crayon picture will show through. This is quite dramatic if bright colored crayons are overwashed with black or brown.

### SCRAPE

Color a small piece of cardboard with two very thick layers of bright crayon. The layers can be the same or two different colors. Then, cover completely with a layer of black crayon. Next, using small scrapers, such as chopsticks or cocktail sticks, scrape away the top layer of crayon to reveal the underlying color or colors.

# String painting

This is another activity that works well with younger and older children alike. However, it is very messy, so have plenty of wet wipes to clean up their hands.

## what to do

Set out two or three saucers of thick paint in various colors, some sheets of drawing paper, and about two to three strings for each saucer.

Make the string brushes by cutting 4–8 in. (10–20 cm) lengths of string or yarn (be sure the strings absorb the paint; some man-made materials do not). To form a handle, pass one end of each string through a piece of macaroni and tie.

Immerse about half the length of the string into the paint. Lift out of the paint and pull it across the paper to make lines and squiggles.

**CHECKLIST**

| age 3–4+ | |
| --- | --- |
| indoor | ✓ |
| no. of children | no limit |
| time | 30 minutes–2 hours |
| help required | ✓ |
| messy | ✓ |

**EQUIPMENT**

- thickened paint (see pages 132–133)
- paper
- saucers
- string or wool
- macaroni
- paper towels, apron, wipes, and floor covering to control mess

## What the child learns

Good for hand–eye coordination, hand skills, and learning to see a task through to a desired end. This is a good painting technique for a child who is clumsy.

# Sticking and gluing

**CHECKLIST**

| | |
|---|---|
| age 2–6 | |
| indoor | ✓ |
| no. of children | no limit |
| time | 20 minutes or more |
| help required | to start |
| messy | ✓ |

**EQUIPMENT**

- flour, water, and food coloring for paste
- wood glue, glue sticks, roll-on glue
- brush or stick to spread
- paper
- items to stick
- paper towels, apron, wipes, and floor covering to control mess

## What the child learns

This is another task that encourages skilled hand movements and good hand–eye coordination. It helps a child to plan, sit still, concentrate, and work toward an end.

Sticking and gluing is another skill that needs to develop gradually. Start by showing the child how to cover the page with paste and drop things onto any part of this surface. Children tend to get confused about where to put the paste when sticking things together, so she will need an occasional reminder.

## what to do

Make a simple paste from flour and water and show the child how to spread it. To make her task easier, add a few drops of food coloring to the paste. Then drop things onto the surface, let it dry, and shake off the excess. Anything light, from split peas, glitter, sequins, eggshells, and cocoa to bits of string or leaves, can be dropped.

Flour paste will not hold heavy items such as dried beans or twigs. Use wood glue for this.

When gluing paper or cloth, coat the back of the item to be stuck on and place it carefully.

Children often find it easier to use a roll-on or stick of glue to stick objects onto a collage. But remember, these do not work well on thin paper.

# Dropping rice

Children of all ages will enjoy this activity. Younger ones will need supervision but older children can be left to work on the various projects by themselves.

## what to do

Cover the paper or oak tag with glue and then drop rice onto it.

Let the paper dry flat, then shake off any excess rice and display it on the wall.

Alternatively, draw a daisy with a ring of petals. Carefully put glue on each petal and drop the rice. Shake off any excess, then cut out a circle from yellow paper and stick it in the middle.

Take a piece of colored paper. Write the child's name on the paper with glue. Let her sprinkle the rice and reveal her name.

Place a saucer or a cup as a template on a piece of paper. Carefully spread glue around it, covering all the paper that is showing. Remove the template and drop the rice. When this is dry, put glue into the area left by the template and drop something else—cocoa powder, instant coffee, or split peas, for example.

| CHECKLIST | |
|---|---|
| age 2+ | |
| indoor | ✓ |
| no. of children | 1–4 |
| time | half a day |
| help required | ✓ |
| messy | ✓ |

**EQUIPMENT**
- paper or oak tag
- wood glue
- pencil
- cup or saucer for template
- various sorts of rice
- cocoa powder, instant coffee, or split peas
- balloon, bag, bowl, jug, funnel, and strainer for more ideas

## What the child learns

Artistic expression, fine-hand control when filling in shapes. Encourages self-confidence.

# More ideas for fun with rice

Put a little rice into a balloon and blow it up. The rice makes the balloon move in unpredictable ways.

Put some rice in a bag, cut off the corner, and use the stream of rice to "draw" a shape.

Experiment with pouring rice into a bowl using a jug, a funnel, and a strainer.

Spread rice over the tabletop and make roads through it.

# Printing with vegetables

This is another activity that works well with younger and older children alike. Potatoes are the classic vegetable used for printing, but there are many other vegetables that can be used.

**CHECKLIST**

| | |
|---|---|
| age 3–6 | |
| indoor | ✓ |
| no. of children | no limit |
| time | 30 minutes–2 hours |
| help required | ✓ |
| messy | ✓ |

**EQUIPMENT**

- thickened paint (see pages 132–133), dish, and paper towels for the pad
- folded newspaper and paper for printing
- vegetables
- potato peeler and knives to cut the vegetables
- paper towels, apron, wipes, and floor covering to control mess

## What the child learns

In common with all artistic activities, printing teaches children that they can make things happen. It improves their fine-finger control and hand–eye coordination. They express themselves artistically and they take pride in their achievement.

# what to do

## SELECTING AND PREPARING

Carrots, sprouts, celery, cabbage, and ears of corn can be cut at various angles to make interesting prints. Avoid fruit that is soft and juicy, although unripe pears and apples work well.

In the fall, look for fallen leaves, walnuts, chestnuts, and little apples from ornamental crab apple trees.

If you skin broad beans, the two halves are easily separated. Slip a large round-headed thumbtack into the side to act as a handle, and print from the flat surface.

Printing from leaf vegetables can get a bit messy, but try the stiff well-textured leaves like cabbage. To avoid frustration, cut the stalks so that the leaves lie flat.

Simple patterns can be cut into the surface of larger root vegetables such as potatoes or turnips. Prepare these for younger children by cutting the vegetable in half and gouging out a simple shape using a sharp knife. An older child can cut a pattern into the surface of a potato with a potato peeler, but do remind him that it is the raised part that will print.

Although it is only possible to print when the painted surface makes contact with the paper, that does not mean that the vegetables you print from must be flat. You can roll on textures. Try picking up paint on half

of a pinecone or an ear of corn and rolling it over the paper. Celery and carrots work, too.

## HOW TO PRINT

First make a printing pad. Place a couple of sheets of paper towel onto a dish and pour on thickened paint.

Dip the vegetable into the paint, stamp test prints on newspaper until the print looks right (there is always too much paint on the vegetables at first), then stamp the paper until the paint runs out. Repeat.

Stamping makes a good all-over pattern, or it can be combined with other techniques.

# Salt dough

**EQUIPMENT**
- flour, salt, glycerine (from a pharmacy), and water for the dough
- rolling pin, blunt knife, and cookie cutters for shaping
- baking sheet lined with foil
- paints and varnish to decorate
- fabric, glue, and yarn for the doll

## What the child learns

Making a model teaches children that they can make things happen. It improves their fine-finger control and hand–eye coordination. It allows them to express themselves artistically and take pride in their achievement.

Salt dough hardens when dried in the oven. It can then be painted and varnished. The end result looks surprisingly professional and keeps for years.

## what to do

### PREPARING THE DOUGH

Mix together three cups of all-purpose flour and one cup of salt. Add just over a cup of water and a tablespoon of glycerine. Knead the dough until it is elastic.

Shape as desired, then place on a baking sheet lined with foil. Bake in a low oven (300°F/150°C) until dry. Flat figures will probably need about

To make Christmas tree decorations, cut out shapes using cookie cutters or a template (a pizza cutter is a useful tool for this). Put a hole in the top for the string and bake. The ornaments can be painted with powder paint and varnished when dry or you could use nail polish.

To make a small doll, roll a ball of salt dough and form it into a head. Take a second smaller ball and roll this to form the neck. Attach it to the head by dampening the surfaces. Bake as above. To make the body, cut a semicircle of fabric, fold it in half, and sew up the seam completely. Cut off the top corner so that it fits the neck, and glue it in place. Wrap yarn around the fabric to secure it to the neck and hide the join.

More elaborate dolls can be made by adding arms and/or making small dough hands and feet, which are stitched into the sides and hem of the dress.

1½ hours, three-dimensional models at least twice that.

Remember, you are drying out the models rather than cooking them, so turn down the oven if the dough starts to brown.

## SALT DOUGH MODELS

A two- to three-year-old will enjoy rolling the dough and cutting it with a blunt knife or cookie cutters. Older children can make more elaborate shapes or three-dimensional models.

# Play dough

**CHECKLIST**

| | |
|---|---|
| age 2–6 | |
| indoor | ✓ |
| no. of children | no limit |
| time | 30 minutes–2 hours |
| help required | to make dough |
| messy | ✓ |

**EQUIPMENT**

- all-purpose flour, salt, water, oil, cream of tartar, food coloring, and a saucepan to make the dough
- rolling pin, blunt knives, cookie cutters, lollipop sticks, hard objects, colander or potato ricer for playing with the dough

## What the child learns

This is the simplest way to make three-dimensional models. It teaches children that they can make things, it improves fine-finger control and hand–eye coordination, and it allows them to express themselves artistically.

Play dough is the ideal material for small children, soft enough to squeeze through the hands, yet firm enough to model with. It does not, however, make lasting models.

## what to do

**MAKING THE DOUGH**

To make play dough, put two cups of flour, one cup of salt, one cup of water, two tablespoons of oil, and two teaspoons of cream of tartar (which makes it last longer) together in a saucepan. Knead and then warm on the stove. It's nice to give the dough to the child while it is still warm. Wrapped in a plastic bag, it will keep for weeks.

Children enjoy making the dough almost as much as they enjoy playing with it. Let them measure the flour and salt and pour in the oil and water as you knead the dough. Then let them knead the dough before you warm it.

To produce a uniform color, add food coloring or powder paint to the water before mixing it into the flour. To make a marbled dough, add the food coloring when you knead the dough.

You can vary this basic recipe to change the texture of the dough. Leave out the oil and you get a more crumbly dough; add a little more oil and the mixture becomes silky. Use self-rising flour and it becomes puffier.

To make a puffy dough that "flows," mix two cups of self-rising flour and a cup of colored water and knead until it is fairly elastic.

## PLAYING WITH THE DOUGH

Give the child a rolling pin, a board, some cookie cutters, a blunt knife, and a lollipop stick, and of course, the dough.

Make impressions in the dough with hard, textured objects such as plastic building bricks, forks, or a potato masher.

Push the dough through a coarse mesh, such as a metal colander or potato ricer, to make "worms."

# Papier mâché

**CHECKLIST**

| | |
|---|---|
| age 4–6+ | |
| indoor | ✓ |
| no. of children | no limit |
| time | 30 minutes to most of a day |
| help required | ✓ |
| messy | ✓ |

**EQUIPMENT**

- newspaper, flour, and water or wood glue for the papier mâché
- large bowl or basin
- bowls, jam jars, glasses, or balloons for molds
- petroleum jelly or plastic wrap
- paint and varnish to decorate
- paper towels, apron, wipes, and floor covering to control mess

## What the child learns

Like all artistic activities, making papier mâché improves a child's fine-finger control and hand–eye coordination and allows him to express himself artistically. Some of these techniques require patience and planning ahead and help children to carry out an activity in an ordered way.

Papier mâché can be used in a number of different ways to make a wide variety of models, from adding shape and dimension to farm or street layouts to making little people or large vases.

## what to do

### MAKING THE PAPIER MÂCHÉ

First, take two or three newspapers and cut or rip them up into strips about 1 in. (2 cm) wide and 3 in. (7 cm) long. Next, partly fill a large bowl with hot water and add the paper. Press down to ensure the strips are thoroughly immersed. Leave them in the water for several hours until they are really soggy and beginning to break up. Squeeze the water out of the paper (whirl it around in a salad spinner if you have one).

Meanwhile, prepare the paste. Either make a simple flour and water paste or use diluted wood glue (one part glue to three parts water). Add the paper to the glue and mix well: It should be as thick as clay. Hands work best for mixing, but be prepared for them to become very sticky!

Papier mâché can be used like clay or play dough to make simple shapes, animals, or small pots. The child could also use it to make terrain for a farm or road layout (see page 216). Let it dry for at least 24 hours before painting and varnishing.

### USING MOLDS

**Molding inside a bowl**

Rub the inside of the mold with petroleum jelly (or cover with plastic wrap) to stop the papier mâché from sticking. Now push the papier mâché up against the sides of the bowl. Let it dry, and then turn it out. It can then be painted and varnished.

## Covering a balloon

Blow up the balloon and cover it with a layer of papier mâché. Let it dry for 24 hours; then add a second layer. Pop the balloon by pushing a pin through the papier mâché once it is dry. These balls make good animals. Adding four legs and a snout (from an egg carton), for example, might make a pig.

## Using paper strips

An alternative (and easier) way to cover a mold is to start by using strips of paper. To make a vase, take a jar or glass and cover the outer surface with a layer of petroleum jelly or plastic wrap. Soak strips of paper in the paste and apply them to the mold one layer at a time, letting each layer dry completely before applying the next. The child can continue in this way until he has the desired thickness, or he can switch to the papier mâché mixture (see above) after a couple of layers. The mold can be removed or left in place (depending on its shape) and the vase painted and varnished.

# Threading

**EQUIPMENT**
- objects to thread, such as empty spools of thread and paper towel tubes, big buttons, macaroni, and straws
- string or clothesline
- paint and paintbrush or fabric and glue
- blunt needle
- scissors

## What the child learns

This is an excellent task for improving fine-finger skills and hand–eye coordination. Making things gives children confidence.

Threading encourages fine-finger control: The hole must be held still with one hand while the thread is guided through accurately with the other. Fortunately, success is easily measured by the number of articles on the string—an altogether satisfactory state of affairs.

## what to do

Two-year-olds like to drag something behind them, and that something can be made easily—from cardboard cylinders, empty toilet paper rolls, or even an old pair of sandals. If it has a hole, he can thread it on to a string.

Make a snake by threading empty spools of thread on to a length of vinyl-covered clothesline. Alternatively, paint the tubes from empty paper towel and toilet paper rolls, or cover them with fabric and thread these on to a length of string to make the snake.

Older children can thread big buttons using a blunt needle. Get them to make bracelets from little chunks of painted macaroni or plastic straws cut into short sections.

# Getting ready to sew

Sewing is a bit tricky for a preschool child because there are so many things that need to be done at the same time. If you keep the tasks simple, you can prepare the groundwork.

## what to do

Make or buy some simple sewing cards. Cut some thin oak tag into squares and draw a large simple shape—a teddy bear or a rabbit, for example. Make pairs of holes, not too far apart, in the oak tag with a hole punch or a skewer. The child then uses a large, blunt needle to sew between the holes. It is easier to sew with yarn than thread, and there are fewer problems if you double the yarn and tie a knot in it.

Craft shops sell mesh that can be used for simple stitching. Mark the holes to be used with a felt-tipped pen.

Felt is the easiest material to use for "real" sewing. Use a short darning needle and a fairly short double thread. Make the first stitch for the child and show her how to pull all the thread through before making the next stitch.

**CHECKLIST**

| age 4+ | |
|---|---|
| indoor | ✓ |
| no. of children | 1 |
| time | 30 minutes |
| help required | ✓ |
| no mess | ✓ |

**EQUIPMENT**
- oak tag, pencil, and hole punch or skewer to make sewing cards
- yarn
- large, blunt needle
- sewing mesh and felt-tipped pen
- felt fabric, darning needle, and thread

## What the child learns
This is an excellent task for improving fine-finger skills and hand–eye coordination, and for preplanning what has to be done next.

# Weaving

**CHECKLIST**

age 3–4+

| | |
|---|---|
| indoor | ✓ |
| no. of children | no limit |
| time | 30 minutes or more |
| help required | ✓ |
| no mess | ✓ |

**EQUIPMENT**

- shoe box
- yarn
- a small piece of cardboard

## What the child learns

This is an excellent task for improving fine-finger skills and hand–eye coordination, and for giving the child pride in what she is able to do. It also teaches her to sit quietly and concentrate, an essential skill for school.

Weaving is fun for children of all ages. Even a three- to four-year-old can manage to weave yarn back and forth in a weaving box. She may not be able to do much with the cloth, but at this age it is not the point.

## what to do

Take a shoe box and punch six holes across each of the longer sides. Cut three long pieces of yarn and thread each one across the box and back and tie it off. You should now have a box with six strings. Now take a longer piece of yarn and wrap it around a small piece of cardboard for the bobbin.

To weave, unwind a little yarn from the bobbin and tie it to the first string. Pass it over and under the strands of yarn in the weaving box. Pull the yarn through, then turn back and repeat from the other side, unwinding yarn as required. Show the child how to straighten the weaving with her fingers (an afro comb works well, too).

When the bobbin runs out, wind more yarn onto it and tie the new string to the old one.

# Let's knit!

Although you have to concentrate and you need to be well coordinated, knitting is a simple repetitive activity. Once children get the hang of it, they can make simple garments such as a teddy bear's scarf.

## what to do

Choose short fat needles and thick yarn. Cast on for the child and then do the first row. Let her sit on your lap and join in by passing the yarn around the needles. Then help her to push the needle through the loop for the next stitch. Proceed in this way for a row or two, letting the child do more and more of the activity herself.

Then let her try by herself. She is bound to get frustrated at first, but most dexterous five-year-olds will master the task in a few sessions. Cast off for her. A square will make a little blanket and a long string ten stitches wide makes a scarf for one of her dolls.

**CHECKLIST**

| | |
|---|---|
| age 4–6 | |
| indoor | ✓ |
| no. of children | 1 |
| time | 30 minutes or more |
| help required | ✓ |
| no mess | ✓ |

**EQUIPMENT**
- large knitting needles
- thick yarn

## What the child learns

This is another excellent task for improving fine-finger skills and hand–eye coordination, and for giving the child pride in what she is able to do. It also encourages her to sit quietly and concentrate, an essential skill for school.

# Making a batik

To make traditional batik, hot wax is painted onto fabric before it is dyed. Obviously, painting with hot wax is much too dangerous for small children. Using flour paste instead is safe and, although the images are not as sharp, the slightly smudged, cracked images have a rustic charm all of their own.

## What to do

Start by making a thick paste of flour and water. Add a tiny drop of food coloring to the paste so that when the child starts he can see which areas are already painted. Pin a piece of good-quality cotton cloth to a board, or stretch it out and fit it to the board with masking tape.

Using a stiff paintbrush, paint a design onto this cloth with the flour paste. You can also sponge, flick, or drip paste over the surface of the cloth, but make sure the covered areas are quite thickly coated.

Alternatively, make templates from paper or oak tag. Parents will probably need to cut the oak tag for younger children, although older children can help make them. The child could paste around objects such as plates, or cut out pictures from magazines and stick them onto a piece of oak tag that she then pastes around. To do this, put the template on the surface of the cloth and put a thick layer of paste over the space that is left uncovered. Allow the cloth to dry thoroughly in a warm place.

Then, carefully following the instructions on the packet, dye the cloth using a cold-water dye. If you start with a light color, the whole process can be repeated with a second color.

### CHECKLIST

| | |
|---|---|
| age 5–6 | |
| indoor | ✓ |
| no. of children | no limit |
| time | 30 minutes–2 hours |
| help required | ✓ |
| messy | ✓ |

### EQUIPMENT

- flour, water, and food coloring for the paste
- good-quality cotton cloth
- board
- pins or masking tape
- stiff paintbrush or sponge
- oak tag or paper and scissors to make templates (optional)
- cold-water dye
- paper towels, apron, wipes, and floor covering to control mess

## What the child learns

Good for hand–eye coordination, hand skills, and learning to see a task through to a desired end. It makes very attractive patterns, and this gives the child a lot of confidence.

# Sand patterns

Many of the techniques in this chapter can be carried out on a tray or tabletop and this one is no exception. If you want to keep a more permanent record, drop the sand onto a sheet of paper that has been liberally covered with wood glue.

## What to do

Make a large cone from oak tag with a small hole at the apex, and attach string to the top so that the cone can be swung from side to side.

Suspend the cone from the edge of a table or from a shelf (it is easiest to hang it from a hook). Place a large tray covered in dark paper underneath the cone. Put your finger over the hole and fill the cone with dry sand, sugar, or salt.

The child then knocks and swings the cone in various directions to make sand patterns.

To stop the flow, put a mug underneath the cone to catch the sand. Put the sand back in the cone when the child wants to start again.

Use a glue stick to draw on the paper before the child starts to swing the cone. Investigate what happens if water lines are painted on the paper.

**CHECKLIST**

| | |
|---|---|
| age 4–6 | |
| indoor/outdoor | ✓ |
| no. of children | no limit |
| time | 10 minutes–1 hour |
| help required | ✓ |
| messy | ✓ |

**EQUIPMENT**
- tray or table
- oak tag
- string
- sand, salt, or sugar
- sheets of dark paper
- glue stick

## What the child learns
To make things happen, to experiment with small changes, to take pride in what he has produced.

# Snipping and cutting

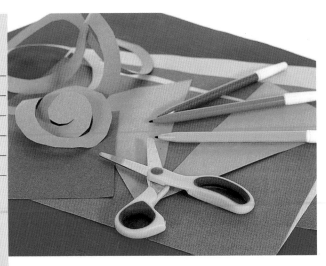

**CHECKLIST**

| | |
|---|---|
| age 2–4+ | |
| indoor | ✓ |
| no. of children | no limit |
| time | 10 minutes or more |
| help required | ✓ |
| messy | ✓ |

**EQUIPMENT**
- blunt-ended scissors
- paper
- newspaper
- colored paste (optional)

## What the child learns

The skilled use of tools is a slow and difficult process; but once achieved, fine-finger and hand control will be enhanced and hand–eye coordination will have improved. The child will find it easier to transfer to that all-important tool, the pen.

While we tend to think "real tools" are much too difficult for preschoolers to use, we have few qualms in offering them what is perhaps the most difficult tool of all: scissors. Blunt-ended scissors are safer for small children to use.

## what to do

**CONTROLLING THE SCISSORS**

Cutting something out requires three skills: the use of the scissors to make a cut, the moving forward of the scissors to make another cut in front of the first, and the directing of the scissors to cut in the desired place. The combination of these skills needs to be built up in the way that any tool-using skill is built up.

Start by teaching the child to snip, to make a single cut. Give her narrow strips of paper (not too thin or floppy) and let her cut them into pieces to make confetti. Gradually make these wider so that she needs to make two, then three snips. She will enjoy dropping these pieces onto a sheet of paper that has been covered with a layer of paste (add some food coloring or powder paint to the paste to make it more visible).

## CONTROLLING THE PAPER

Teach the child to make small, then gradually longer rips in a sheet of newspaper. Small children find this mundane task surprisingly enjoyable.

Once this is mastered, progress to ripping strips of paper, then ripping around corners, and finally, to ripping around a picture. Practice by drawing wiggly lines and seeing if she can follow them.

## PUTTING IT ALL TOGETHER

Once she has learned to control the scissors and the paper, she is ready to put the two tasks together. Start by drawing lines for her to snip with the scissors.

# Just fold some paper

Preschool children in Japan are well versed in paper folding; it is excellent practice for making precise hand movements. The secret is to fold carefully and to run a fingernail along the creases to make sure they are sharp.

## CHECKLIST

| | |
|---|---|
| age 4+ | |
| indoor/outdoor | ✓ |
| no. of children | no limit |
| time | 10 minutes to make, 30 minutes to play |
| help required | ✓ |
| no mess | ✓ |

## EQUIPMENT

- paper
- adhesive tape
- pencil
- scissors
- powder paint or felt-tip pens

## What the child learns

To follow instructions to the letter. To make precise hand movements.

## PAPER AIRPLANE

Fold a sheet of paper in half lengthwise. Make a sharp crease. Unfold and lay flat, with the outside of the crease facing up.

Fold the top corners over to meet the central crease, then fold each side again to meet the central crease. Repeat until you can't fold the paper any more.

Now fold the plane back in half along the first crease. Open out the wings and place a small piece of adhesive tape fore and aft to hold the fuselage together.

Write the destinations on the wing of each plane and see how far they will fly.

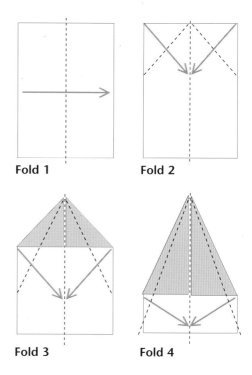

Fold 1     Fold 2

Fold 3     Fold 4

## PAPER HAT

Fold a piece of paper in half widthwise and make a sharp crease. Fold in half again, then unfold and smooth out flat.

Now fold the top corners down to meet the center crease. Fold the bottom flap up, turn the paper over, and do the same with the other bottom flap.

Carefully pull apart the bottom edges to complete your hat. Decorate the hat using powder paints or felt-tip pens.

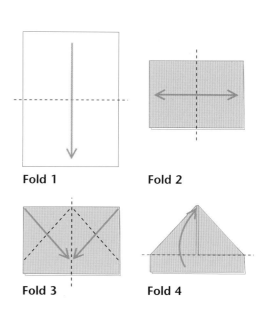

Fold 1     Fold 2

Fold 3     Fold 4

# boisterous

✳ Throwing and aiming

✳ Bop until you drop

✳ Musical statues

✳ Traffic lights

✳ Hiding and finding games

✳ Chasing games

✳ Blow football

✳ Obstacle course

✳ Water spouts

✳ Bowling

✳ Shark-infested water

✳ Flowerpot stilts

✳ Through the arches

✳ Head and shoulders

✳ Follow the leader

✳ Follow the rope

✳ A relay race

games

# Throwing and aiming

age 3–6

| | |
|---|---|
| indoor/outdoor | ✓ |
| no. of children | no limit |
| time | 10 minutes–1 hour |
| help required | to start |
| no mess | ✓ |

**EQUIPMENT**

- newspaper, socks, foam balls, paper airplanes and beanbags for throwing
- buckets and shopping bags for catching
- rice, beans, or styrofoam chips and small freezer bags for beanbags
- source of music

## What the child learns

Improves aiming and throwing skills. Good for hand–eye coordination and spatial skills. Playing and laughing together forges friendships.

Even in a small room it's possible to practice throwing, providing you use a ball of scrunched-up newspaper and clear away breakable items. In the yard you can use a real ball, but remember that a soft foam ball or beanbag is easier to hold with one hand, and that makes throwing and aiming simpler for the younger age groups.

## what to do

### GAMES TO ENCOURAGE THROWING

Make balls out of newspaper and practice throwing these. If you have two children, let them have a newspaper fight. Give each child an armchair that you load with paper balls, and let them throw them around the room or at each other's chair.

Collect old socks, roll them into balls, and put them in a bucket at one end of the room (or out in the hall). Put on some music and let the children dance around. As soon as the music stops, they rush to the bucket and throw socks until the music starts again. They then have to pick up the socks and put them back in the bucket before the game starts all over again!

### GAMES THAT PRACTICE AIMING
### Human bowling

This is a great game for a party. Collect a pile of socks and make them into balls. Divide the children into throwers and bowling pins. The bowling pins stand at one end of the room with their backs to the throwers. The throwers try to hit the pins. When they are hit, the pins fall over (with great drama, of course!). When all the pins are down, the two teams switch roles.

## Catch and throw darts

One player, the thrower, has a pile of paper airplanes (see page 167) while the other, the catcher, has a shopping bag in which to catch the airplanes. Start the music. The thrower throws; the catcher tries to catch. The aim is to see how many airplanes can be caught before the music stops.

## Beanbags

Heavy beanbags are easier to aim than light ones. Put some rice into a small freezer bag and roll it up in a sock to make an instant beanbag. You could try other fillings such as dried beans or styrofoam chips.

# Bop until you drop

**CHECKLIST**

| | |
|---|---|
| age 2–5 | |
| indoor/outdoor | ✓ |
| no. of children | no limit |
| time | 10 minutes |
| no help required | ✓ |
| no mess | ✓ |

**EQUIPMENT**

- source of music
- dust rags (optional)

## What the child learns

This is not so much a learning activity as a learning enabler. Not only does it allow the child to settle down to a sustained and more demanding activity, it also serves as a cue for the "right frame of mind" for such activities.

Before a child can settle down to a sustained activity, he needs to let off steam. This is especially true for the under-fives. A quick bop around the room releases the pent-up energy that otherwise leads to fidgeting, which can spoil the child's concentration.

## what to do

Put on the music, and dance. If you have a floor that needs polishing, tie dust rags onto the children's feet and let their feet do the polishing!

This is also an excellent start to the wind down before bedtime. Follow it with a relaxing bath, a story, and a warm milky drink.

# I can do the cancan

This is another activity that encourages children to let off steam. It's best played with more than one child. Ideal as a last game before refreshments at a party, it can be played indoors or outdoors.

If there are more than six children, divide them into two groups. Each group can sing and carry out the actions alternately; otherwise, let all the children do all of the actions together.

The children stand facing each other and sing the first line together; then they alternate. Their actions should always match their words.

*I can do the cancan just like this*
*I can do the hoola hoop*
*I can do the twist*
*Queens all curtsy*
*Kings all bow.*
*Boys shout "Hi there"*
*Girls go "WOW."*

# Dead lions

In the middle of the boisterous excitement of a party, this change of pace is a firm favorite for parents and party-goers alike. It's best played with a group of children, but you could play it with one child.

The aim of dead lions is to stay "dead" still for as long as possible. All but one player lie down on the ground and try not to move a muscle. Breathing is allowed, of course, but absolutely nothing else. The "looker" is joined by any children caught moving. The game continues until there is only one child left on the ground.

# Musical statues

**CHECKLIST**

| | |
|---|---|
| age 3–6 | |
| indoor/outdoor | ✓ |
| no. of children | no limit |
| time | 10 minutes or more |
| help required | ✓ |
| no mess | ✓ |

**EQUIPMENT**

- source of music
- chairs
- cushions

## What the child learns

To enjoy playing together with other children. Moving to music encourages her to learn its rhyme and rhythm. It's a good way to let off steam.

These four traditional children's games, all based around the same theme, can be played by any number of children. A child can dance around on her own to expend some energy before bed, or with half-a-dozen friends as a party game. Start by selecting an open dancing space and some music.

## what to do

**MUSICAL STATUES**

The children dance around until the music is turned off. They must then hold exactly the position they were in when the music stopped. A picker (the parent) touches all those seen moving and they then join in looking for movements. As soon as the last child moves, the music starts again.

## MUSICAL BUMPS

Children dance around bumping bottoms or hips whenever they meet. When the music stops, all the children sit down. The last one to sit down is out. The game continues until there is only one child left.

## MUSICAL TUMBLES

Put a pile of cushions in one corner and put on some music for the children to dance to. When they dance past the cushions, stop the music. The children then tumble onto the cushions.

## MUSICAL CHAIRS

Arrange a row of chairs, alternating each chair so that it faces the opposite way. There should be one chair less than the number of children playing. The children dance around the chairs to the music. When the music stops, the children sit down on a chair. The child left standing is out. Continue the game until there is only one child left—and don't forget to take away a chair each time!

# Traffic lights

## EQUIPMENT

none required

## What the child learns

To enjoy playing together with other children. To anticipate what people are going to do next (an important skill from the age of four). These are good party games. Like most traditional games, they encourage cooperation rather than competition: The fun is in the playing, not the winning!

Traditional children's games have been tried and tested by generations. They survive because they allow children to come together and play with few formalities. The games here encourage children to observe and predict what other children are doing.

## what to do

### RED LIGHT, GREEN LIGHT

One person is chosen to be the traffic light. He stands out front with his back to the other children. He then shouts "green light," and everyone creeps forward to try and touch the traffic light. From time to time the traffic light shouts "red light" and spins around. Everyone must stand absolutely still. Anyone caught moving becomes the traffic light for the next game.

Grandmother's Footsteps is a very similar game, except that "grandmother" does not give any warning before she turns.

### TRAFFIC LIGHTS

One player is chosen to be "It" and shouts out the instructions. The last person to start the action is out. Players are also out if they do the wrong action. The last player to be out is It next time.

If It shouts RED, everyone must stand still.

If It shouts GREEN, they must run around.

If It shouts CRASH, everyone lies on the ground.

If It shouts BRIDGE, everyone must bend over and make an arch.

If It shouts TRAFFIC JAM, everyone must creep along as slowly as possible.

# Hiding and finding games

Games of hide-and-seek in various forms have been around for many generations, their longevity a testament to their enduring popularity. Here are a few variations on the theme.

## what to do

### HIDE-AND-SEEK
In the basic game, one person is chosen to be "It." He hides his face and counts or says a rhyme while the others run away and hide. The seeker then shouts "Here I come, ready or not" and goes to look for everyone. The last (or the first) player to be found plays It for the next round.

### TOAD IN THE HOLE
In this variation, if you are found you join the seeker looking for the other players.

### CUCKOO
In this game, only one player hides and everyone else seeks.

### SARDINES
In this game, one person hides and everyone goes in search of him. If they find the sardine, they hide with him. The game continues until everyone is huddled into the hiding place.

### BUG AND RUG
In this game, if you are found you can run "home" and if you can get there without being caught, you are safe. In other variations you can run home when it is safe even before you are spotted.

**CHECKLIST**

| | |
|---|---|
| age 3–6 | |
| indoor/outdoor | ✓ |
| no. of children | 3 or more |
| time | half a day |
| help required | ✓ |
| no mess | ✓ |

**EQUIPMENT**
none required

## What the child learns
To understand and abide by simple rules. To enjoy playing together with other children. To anticipate what people are going to do next. The fun is in the playing, not the winning!

# Chasing games

**CHECKLIST**

| | |
|---|---|
| age 3–6 | |
| outdoor | ✓ |
| no. of children | 6 or more |
| time | 10 minutes or more |
| help required | ✓ |
| no mess | ✓ |

**EQUIPMENT**

none required

## What the child learns

To enjoy playing together with other children, to anticipate what other children are doing (an important skill for a four-year-old). These are good party games in which the fun is in the playing, not the winning!

Another old-fashioned favorite, chasing games allow children to play together with few formalities. These two energetic games require children to observe and predict what other children will do. Both need at least six players.

## what to do

### CROWS AND CRANES

Divide the children into two teams: the Crows and the Cranes. If there is an odd number, the extra child becomes the caller; if not, an adult can be the caller.

The teams line up on opposite sides of the yard, each behind a line. When the caller shouts "walk," they walk toward each other.

The caller then shouts either "Crow" or "Crane," and the team that is named must chase the other team back to their line. Any player who is caught joins the catcher's side. The game ends when there is no one left on one of the teams. The caller can make things more interesting by shouting "Crrrrrrrrrrrrrrrrrrrr-anes!" or "Crrrrrrrrrrrrrrr-ows!"

## FOX AND GEESE

One player is chosen to be the farmer and another to be the fox. An adult can be the farmer if there are not many children, but a child has to play the fox. The rest of the players are the geese. The farmer takes the geese to their pasture, then goes back to his house. The fox skulks between the farmer and the geese.

The farmer shouts:
"Geese, geese, come home"
but the geese reply:
"No. We are frightened of Mr. Fox."
The farmer then shouts:
"Mr. Fox has gone away, and won't be back today. Geese, geese, come home."

The geese must try to run home, and the fox tries to catch one of them. The game can continue until all the geese are caught, with the first child caught becoming the fox, and the last one the farmer, or they can just change roles after each round of play.

# Blow football

**CHECKLIST**

| | |
|---|---|
| age 3–6 | |
| indoor | ✓ |
| no. of children | 1–2 |
| time | 10 minutes or more |
| help required | to start |
| no mess | ✓ |

**EQUIPMENT**

- table
- a shoebox cut in half, scissors, and adhesive gum for the goals
- Ping-Pong ball
- 2 straws

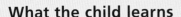

## What the child learns

Playing and laughing together forges friendships. Breath control and spatial skills improve, too.

This is a simple game for two children to play, or for you to play with the child. All you need is a table, a Ping-Pong ball, a couple of straws, and two goals.

### what to do

A shoebox cut in half will make good goals. Lie each half cut-side-down and fix them to opposite sides of the table with adhesive gum.

Give each child a straw and let him blow through it to move the ball. The aim is to blow the ball into the opposite goal and stop it from entering his own goal.

# Obstacle course

This is an all-time favorite for the under-fives, and especially good when a child needs cheering up. Be warned, if you have a group of children playing, it can get a bit out of hand.

## what to do

Put a pile of cushions at the bottom of the stairs and let the child jump. To avert disaster in the shape of broken bones, set a limit on the number of steps she is allowed to jump, and watch her closely. Alternatively, she could jump off the bed or sofa onto pillows and quilts.

Hold the child's hand while she walks along a low wall and jumps off at the end.

Walk the plank. Put a builder's plank (or a couple of wooden shelves) between two bricks and let the child walk the plank and jump off the end.

**CHECKLIST**

| | |
|---|---|
| age 3–4+ | |
| indoor/outdoor | ✓ |
| no. of children | no limit |
| time | 10 minutes or more |
| help required | supervision |
| no mess | ✓ |

**EQUIPMENT**
- stairs, bed, or sofa
- cushions or pillows and quilts
- low wall
- planks or shelves
- bricks

## What the child learns

Jumping improves breath control, fitness, and spatial skills. If another child is involved, playing and laughing together forges friendship.

# Water spouts

**CHECKLIST**

age 3–6

| | |
|---|---|
| outdoor/indoor | ✓ |
| no. of children | no limit |
| time | 10 minutes to half a day |
| help required | ✓ |
| messy | ✓ |

**EQUIPMENT**

- water
- hose, sprinkler, wading pool
- bath toys
- balloons
- lollipop sticks
- plastic plates
- Ping-Pong balls
- bucket

## What the child learns

Running, dodging, and avoiding are important physical skills. Laughing together cements friendships.

There is nothing quite like water to produce excitement in children. Maybe it's the way water captures the light, or just the feel of water on the skin, but a warm day, a sprinkler, and a group of children is a surefire recipe for an afternoon of laughter and glee.

## what to do

Get out the hose, turn it to a fine spray, and chase the children around the yard. Alternatively, move the spray as if it was a jump rope, and get them to jump over it.

Set up a sprinkler and let the children run in and out of the stream of water.

Get out the wading pool and the bath toys and let them play (but keep a close eye on them).

Put a little water into some balloons and watch how they wobble.

Play Pooh sticks (racing lollipop sticks) in the wading pool. Drop in the sticks and show each child how to use a plastic plate (or an open hand) to agitate the water behind his stick. This can also be played in the bath.

Partly fill a bucket with water and give the child two or three Ping-Pong balls. He takes a ball and, holding it firmly, plunges his hand underwater; then he lets the ball go so that it shoots up. This can be played in the bath, too.

# Bowling

Balls are unsuitable for throwing in confined spaces indoors. Scrunched-up newspaper can be used instead, and even then it is wise to clear away breakable items. But if the child is intent on a ball game, bowling is a safer option because the ball is rolled, not thrown.

## what to do

You can buy plastic bowling pins, but sealed plastic bottles partly filled with colored water make excellent homemade alternatives. Adjust the amount of water in the bottle to suit the ball used and the age of the child. The lighter the pin, the easier it is to topple, and the less forceful the throw needed. You can decorate the bottles if you wish.

Paint with a coat of diluted wood glue (one part glue to four parts water) to form a key for the paint to stick to, and then paint or decorate with felt-tipped pens.

Set up the pins, draw a bowling line or lines (older children roll the ball from further away), take aim, and roll the ball. The aim is to knock over all of the pins in as few throws as possible.

**CHECKLIST**

| | |
|---|---|
| age 3–4+ | |
| indoor/outdoor | ✓ |
| no. of children | no limit |
| time | 10 minutes or more |
| help required | to start |
| no mess | ✓ |

**EQUIPMENT**
- plastic screw-top bottles, water, and food coloring (optional), to make bowling pins
- ball
- diluted wood glue, paint, paintbrush or felt-tipped pens to decorate (optional)

## What the child learns

To aim with increasing accuracy. Bowling also improves the child's spatial awareness and spatial skills.

# Shark-infested water

## CHECKLIST

age 4–6

| | |
|---|---|
| indoor/outdoor | ✓ |
| no. of children | no limit |
| time | 10 minutes or more |
| help required | ✓ |
| no mess | ✓ |

## EQUIPMENT

- newspaper, paper plates, house bricks, or terra-cotta plant pots for stepping-stones
- low walls
- paths made from cardboard (optional)

## What the child learns

This is an excellent game for developing balance. It is also a fun activity that gets a group of children laughing and joking—great for developing social skills.

This is another good game for improving and developing balancing skills while having fun.

## what to do

Set out some "stepping-stones." For younger children, use paper plates or some folded newspaper; for older children, house bricks and/or upturned plant pots will suffice (but keep an eye on them). They should be placed close enough for the child to be able to step on them, but far enough apart to be a challenge.

The child's task is simple. The sea is infested with sharks, and the only way across is to step on the stepping-stones. One foot in the water and the sharks will bite.

You can turn the stepping-stones into a real obstacle course by including low garden walls, narrow paths made from strips of cardboard, and barriers that he must climb over or duck under.

# Flowerpot stilts

**CHECKLIST**

| | |
|---|---|
| age 5–6 | |
| indoor/outdoor | ✓ |
| no. of children | no limit |
| time | 10 minutes or more |
| help required | to make stilts |
| no mess | ✓ |

**EQUIPMENT**

- 2 plastic flowerpots
- tape measure
- string
- scissors
- skewer to make holes

## What the child learns

This is great for developing balance. It also fosters laughing and joking, which is good for developing social skills.

You can buy small stilts for young children, but they are simple to make yourself from plastic flowerpots.

## what to do

Ask the child to hold his hands by his sides and measure the distance from the child's hand to his foot. Cut two pieces of string, each one just over twice this length.

Select two plastic flowerpots of the same size and make two holes with a skewer—one on either side just below the rim. Poke the string through each hole and tie a knot to secure in place.

The child stands on the upturned flowerpots, holds the string, and walks.

# Through the arches

## CHECKLIST

age 3–6

| | |
|---|---|
| indoor/outdoor | ✓ |
| no. of children | 6 or more |
| time | 10 minutes or more |
| help required | ✓ |
| no mess | ✓ |

## EQUIPMENT

• source of music (optional)

## What the child learns

To enjoy playing with other children. The rhyme and rhythm of the songs encourage the child to hear the little sounds that make up words, which is excellent for later reading and spelling.

These two games both need about six players. As with other traditional games, they remain a popular way for children to come together and play with little formality.

## what to do

### London Bridge

Two players (silver and gold, decided secretly) join hands and form an arch. The other children line up to go under the bridge. They sing this song.

*London Bridge is falling down,*
  *falling down, falling down,*
*London Bridge is falling down,*
  *My fair lady.*

ACTION: ON "MY FAIR LADY," THE BRIDGE FALLS AND CAPTURES A PRISONER.

## Chorus

*Take a key and lock her/him up,*
  *lock her/him up, lock her/him up,*
*Take a key and lock her/him up,*
  *My fair lady.*

*Build it up with iron bars...*
*Iron bars will bend and break...*
*Build it up with silver and gold...*

ACTION: DURING THE CHORUS, THE BRIDGE GENTLY SWAYS THE PRISONER BACK AND FORTH. AT THE END OF THE CHORUS, THE PRISONER IS SECRETLY ASKED, "DO YOU WANT TO PAY WITH SILVER OR GOLD?" THE PRISONER THEN STANDS BEHIND THE CHILD REPRESENTING HER CHOICE. THE GAME CONTINUES THROUGH ALL VERSES AND CHORUS UNTIL ALL THE CHILDREN HAVE BEEN CAPTURED. Finally, the gold and silver lines have a tug of war until one side is pulled across a central marker.

### In and out the windows

One child is chosen to be the dancer. The rest of the children stand in a circle, holding hands and lifting up their arms to make a series of arches. This can be played to music if you wish.

The dancer dances in and out of the arches. She then stops in front of another player, which indicates that player is to join her weaving in and out of the arches. The new partner leads while the dancer follows.

They skip round the circle once, stopping when they reach the partner's place. Here they bow to each other, the dancer takes the partner's place, and the partner becomes the new dancer.

The game begins again.

# Head and shoulders

## CHECKLIST

| | |
|---|---|
| age 3–4+ | |
| indoor/outdoor | ✓ |
| no. of children | no limit |
| time | 10 minutes or more |
| help required | ✓ |
| no mess | ✓ |

## EQUIPMENT

none required

## What the child learns

To enjoy playing together with other children. The rhyme and rhythm of the song also encourage the child to hear the little sounds that make up words, which is excellent for later reading and spelling.

This is another action song, or chant. It's great for a party or just to fill in an odd moment while you wait for something else to happen.

## what to do

### Head and Shoulders

ACTION: THE CHILDREN SING (OR CHANT) THE WORDS, TOUCHING THE NAMED BODY PART EACH TIME THEY MENTION (OR MIME) IT.

*Head and shoulders, knees and toes, knees and toes.*
*Head and shoulders, knees and toes, knees and toes.*
*And eyes, and ears, and mouth and nose,*
*Head and shoulders, knees and toes, knees and toes.*

ACTION: IN THE SECOND VERSE, THEY DO NOT SAY "HEAD," BUT CONTINUE TO POINT TO IT.

*... and shoulders, knees and toes, knees and toes.*
*... and shoulders, knees and toes, knees and toes.*
*And eyes, and ears, and mouth and nose*
*... and shoulders, knees and toes, knees and toes.*

ACTION: THEY CONTINUE SINGING, LEAVING OFF THE NEXT BODY PART ON THE LIST WITH EACH SUCCESSIVE VERSE, BUT CONTINUING TO POINT TO IT. THE NINTH AND FINAL VERSE GOES LIKE THIS:

*... and ..., ... and ..., ... and ....*
*... and ..., ... and ..., ... and ....*
*And ..., and ..., and ... and ...,*
*... and ..., ... and ..., ... and ....*

# Follow the leader

Children have always enjoyed "Follow-the-leader" games. The first of these is simple enough to be suitable for the youngest age group, while the second, Ayah Ayah Conga, is much loved by five- to six-year-olds.

## what to do
### Follow the Leader

ACTION: ONE CHILD IS THE LEADER, THE NEXT HOLDS ON TO HER CLOTHING—OR A ROPE—AND SO ON UNTIL THE CHILDREN ARE ALL LINKED. THEY MUST ALL DO WHAT THE LEADER DOES, SUCH AS PUTTING HER HAND UP, SITTING DOWN, OR TOUCHING HER TOES. THEY CAN SKIP AROUND WHILE THE MUSIC PLAYS OR CHANT AND SHOUT.

*We're following the leader, leader, leader*
*We're following the leader*
*Wherever she may go. (Whatever she may do.)*

**CHECKLIST**

| | |
|---|---|
| age 2–6 | |
| indoor/outdoor | ✓ |
| no. of children | no limit |
| time | 20 minutes or more |
| help required | ✓ |
| no mess | ✓ |

**EQUIPMENT**
• source of music (optional)

## What the child learns
To enjoy playing together with other children. To copy actions.

# Ayah Ayah Conga

This is similar, but here children form a chain by each putting their arms around the waist of the child in front. They all shout "ayah ayah conga" as they snake from room to room. It is too difficult for the youngest children, but the over-fives really enjoy it.

# Follow the rope

| | |
|---|---|
| age 3–6 | |
| outdoor | ✓ |
| no. of children | no limit |
| time | 10 minutes or more |
| help required | to start |
| no mess | ✓ |

**EQUIPMENT**
- 2 jump ropes

## What the child learns
To enjoy physical activities and be fit and healthy. To have fun with other children. To respond to instructions.

Skipping is probably too difficult for all but the most agile five- to six-year-olds, but these are a few rope games that do not involve skipping. They can all be played by only one child or a group of children.

## what to do

### Follow the Snake

Place the jump rope on the ground like a snake. The child walks along its back. The rhyme is optional.

*Two, four, six, eight, Johnny saw a rattlesnake,*
*Eating cake by the lake; two, four, six, eight.*

# High Low

This game is better with several children. Two people hold the rope. If they hold it high and shout *under the stars*, everyone runs under the rope. When they shout *over the moon* they hold the rope low and everyone jumps. Sometimes the jumps are high, and sometimes it is necessary for them to slither under the rope on their tummies.

# Between the ropes

Make two parallel lines on the ground with jump ropes. The child hops from one to the other, and when she has managed to get to the end, the gap is widened and she tries again. Again, the rhyme is optional.

*Hippity hop to the candy shop,*
*to buy a stick of candy.*
*One for you and one for me and*
*one for my sister Sandy.*

# A relay race

| | |
|---|---|
| indoor/outdoor | ✓ |
| no. of children | no limit |
| time | 10 minutes–1 hour |
| help required | ✓ |
| no mess | ✓ |

**EQUIPMENT**

- *all optional:* paper plates, ropes, cardboard boxes, hoops, balls, buckets, steps, pillowcases, scarves for tying legs and blindfolds, trampoline, climbing frame

## What the child learns

To balance, aim, and make precise movements. To understand spatial relationships and enjoy physical activities. To be, and remain, fit and healthy.

Building or doing jigsaws are not the only way of developing a child's spatial abilities. An obstacle course or a relay race, involving finding his way around and throwing and aiming, helps a child orient his body in space and understand how things move in relation to his body. It is also great fun and enables a child (or, more especially, a group of children) to let off steam in readiness for periods of sustained concentration on quieter activities.

## what to do

A relay race consists of a number of activities that can be carried out by one or more children, either in competition against others or themselves. The idea is to have about four to five contrasting activities that build on each other. Here are a few suggestions.

- Running as fast as he can
- Hopping, skipping, or jumping for a short distance (or doing all three in turn)
- Walking in a silly way
- Walking with a blindfold on
- Jumping a small gap
- Crawling on all fours
- Squirming on his tummy
- Rolling over and over down a bank
- Walking on a plank, beam, or small wall
- Stepping on paper plates so that his feet do not touch the floor

- Jumping over a rope
- Rolling under a rope
- Crawling through a large, open cardboard box
- Putting a hoop over his head and then stepping out of it
- Throwing a ball into a bucket
- Balancing a book on his head
- Getting into a pillowcase and jumping along inside it
- Doing somersaults
- Doing bunny hops
- Doing goose steps
- Meeting up with someone to make a wheelbarrow
- Giving another child a piggyback ride
- Having a three-legged race
- Climbing a frame
- Jumping off a step
- Bouncing on a trampoline

# imaginative

* It's my story
* Shoe store
* The corner store
* A trip on a train
* Being you
* Dressing-up box
* Ghosts and monsters
* Water, water
* Just a few big boxes
* Tents
* Picnic
* Tin-can telephone
* Construct
* Roads and other layouts
* Quick and easy puppets

games

# It's my story

CHECKLIST

age 2–6

| | |
|---|---|
| indoor | ✓ |
| no. of children | no limit |
| time | 30 minutes or more |
| help required | to start |
| no mess | ✓ |

EQUIPMENT

- dolls and teddy bears
- scaled-down versions of everyday domestic appliances
- books and videos
- dressing-up clothes
- small toys such as cars or miniature people she can direct

## What the child learns

To remember her experiences and "talk" about her life. To work out why things happen the way they do. To put herself in someone else's shoes.

Imaginative play is the acting out of a story. At an age when it is difficult for children to organize their thoughts into words, children play through their everyday experiences, their worries, and the special things that happen to them. The props of such stories fuel imaginative play.

## what to do

For a child who spends her days at home, props should include toy versions of everyday household equipment such as pots and pans, vacuum cleaners, irons, and brooms.

A child with a baby sister needs a "child" of her own: a doll or teddy bear, diapers, a bottle, a cradle.

A child who has started nursery school needs a whole array of dolls and stuffed animals to attend her nursery school.

There is no point it making a train of boxes for her to play in if she has not been on a train. Give her the experience—take her on a short train ride—and then find the props.

Books and videos tell the stories for her. They become part of her experience and her imaginary games. They teach her how to tell her story.

The conversation around the child is also part of her story. She may not know what "work" is, but she knows that it needs a briefcase and that it cannot be done without high heels and makeup.

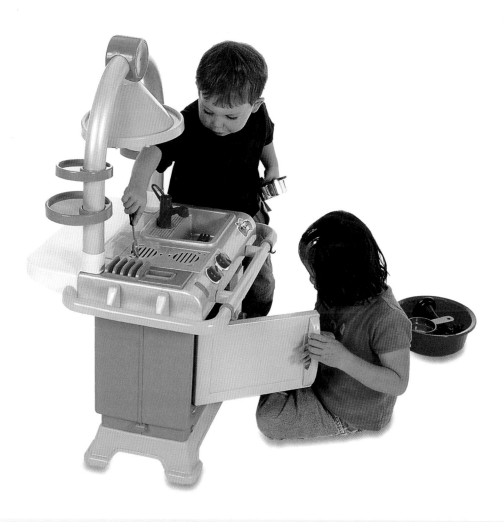

# Little worlds

Sometimes the child is an actor playing a role, and when she plays that role she likes her props to be scaled down but still large. Dolls and teddy bears, for example, can sit in cars.

At other times she is the director: She sits outside the action moving her cars around her roads, taking the little farm animals for a drink.

Sometimes she plays the whole game and needs all the props, while at other times she just wants a little bit of the game. She may want her bride's outfit, even though she is not playing weddings today.

# Shoe store

**CHECKLIST**

| | |
|---|---|
| age 3–4+ | |
| indoor | ✓ |
| no. of children | no limit |
| time | 30 minutes or more |
| help required | to start |
| no mess | ✓ |

**EQUIPMENT**

- shoes and shoe boxes
- chairs or sofa
- piece of oak tag and pencil
- cash register and money
- bags

## What the child learns

To remember experiences and the intricacies of making a purchase. Pretending to be someone else helps a child to think about how it must feel to be someone else.

Recent experiences are what children base their imaginative games on. If the child has recently been to town to buy new shoes, the store she needs today is a shoe store, and the story is all about going to buy them.

## what to do

This is a game to play for the week in which you buy her new shoes. You can start by collecting shoes from around the house and putting them out neatly on a shelf.

Next, line up the dining chairs, or use the sofa, for the customers to sit on. She will also need a piece of oak tag with a pair of feet drawn on it and some numbers so that she can measure feet.

Ask at the shoe store for shoe boxes. After the game is over they make excellent storage boxes for pens and small toys. She will also need a cash register (an empty shoe box will do) and some bags so she can take the money and wrap up the shoes. If you usually pay by credit card, she'll need (a pretend) one of those, too.

# The corner store

Remember to base imaginative games on the child's experience. Going to the corner store or the supermarket, for example, is something you are bound to have done together.

## what to do

Take the child to the corner store—an obvious but vital element. If you always shop at the supermarket, she will need to play supermarket, and the props she needs may be different.

Collect empty packages. These are also useful for making cardboard constructions (see pages 214–215). Let her borrow canned goods, such as beans and tomatoes, for the duration of the game.

She may need some newspapers, bottles of milk, or candy—whatever it is that you usually buy.

She will need a cash register and some money. You can buy pretend money, but I always think it's much easier to turn the cost of the plastic money into small change and use that. Make sure she has bags to put purchases into and some old receipts to give out.

**CHECKLIST**

| | |
|---|---|
| age 3–4+ | |
| indoor | ✓ |
| no. of children | no limit |
| time | 30 minutes or more |
| help required | to start |
| no mess | ✓ |

**EQUIPMENT**
- old food packaging
- cans of food
- newspapers and candy
- cash register and money (small change)
- bags
- old receipts

## What the child learns

To remember her experiences and "talk" about her life. To work out why things happen the way that they do. To put herself in someone else's shoes.

# A trip on a train

| | |
|---|---|
| age 3–4+ | |
| indoor/outdoor | ✓ |
| no. of children | no limit |
| time | 1 hour or more |
| help required | to start |
| no mess | ✓ |

**EQUIPMENT**

- chairs
- soft toys for passengers
- train tickets
- hat and ticket puncher

## What the child learns

To remember her experiences and "talk" about her life. To work out why things happen the way that they do. To put herself in someone else's shoes.

Instead of talking, children play through their everyday experiences. Taking your child on an outing to create the experiences for their imaginitive play does not have to be elaborate to fuel those stories. It just has to be different.

## what to do

The first thing to do is to plan the trip. Talk about trains. Tell the child about buying the ticket, about the platform, and about getting on the train. Go down and look at the station.

Take the child on a trip. It does not need to be far. Two stops on a suburban train is exciting; a three-hour train ride probably is not!

Look for the little details that will make the re-creation of the trip special.

When you get home, sit with the child and talk about her day.

Provide the props for her to play with while the experience is fresh in her mind: a line of chairs for her soft toys to sit on, some tickets, and a hat so she can be the conductor and punch the tickets.

A pretend bus journey will need someone to play the driver, but unless you show her the train engineer, she will be quite oblivious to who is driving the train.

# Being you

For the most part, imaginative play is the playing out of her everyday experiences, and since her family is central to her life, it is inevitably part of her pretence. She may not know precisely what you do at work, but she can see the outward signs, and it is on these that she will base her play.

## what to do

To play at being you, she needs the essential props: glasses, if you wear them, high-heeled shoes, a briefcase, tools, a doctor's bag.

Stand back and look at yourself as you leave the house for work or chores. Do you search for your cell phone? Do you check your briefcase? Do you get in your car? Whatever your rituals are, you will need to provide props.

Talk to her about going to work. Show her people working. You may not have a stamp like the bank teller, or a phone, but if her experience of "work" includes these, she will need them.

Are there hobbies the child will want to act out? Does she need a fishing rod, a football, or a gym bag?

**CHECKLIST**

| | |
|---|---|
| age 3–4+ | |
| indoor | ✓ |
| no. of children | 1 |
| time | 30 minutes or more |
| no help required | ✓ |
| no mess | ✓ |

**EQUIPMENT**
- any props you use

## What the child learns

To work out why things happen the way that they do; to put her thoughts about things into actions. To practice thinking about how it feels to be someone else.

# Dressing-up box

## CHECKLIST

age 3–6

| | |
|---|---|
| indoor/outdoor | ✓ |
| no. of children | no limit |
| time | 30 minutes or more |
| help required | ✓ |
| no mess | ✓ |

## EQUIPMENT

- special outfits and props (e.g., wings and wands)
- old clothes
- old shoes, gloves, hats, glasses, bags, jewelry
- mesh curtains
- material, scissors, velcro, needle and thread for tunic

## What the child learns

By acting at being someone else children begin to realize that other people do not share their thoughts and feelings. That knowledge has a profound effect on how the child interacts with people. The surer he becomes of this, the less open he becomes. He learns to hide his feelings.

Most preschoolers love dressing up. Sometimes they dress up to play a game, and this is almost always the case when they are playing with other children. But when children are playing by themselves they may just like to wear the costume.

## what to do

### SPECIAL OUTFITS TO BUY

Most boys want to be a superhero; most girls want a glittery glamorous outfit. Sexist it may be, but at this age, that's the point. Children are trying to learn what it is that they will grow up to be—what women are, or men are, that the other gender is not. In today's unisex world, it's more difficult than it used to be, and children grab on to the few absolutes—the high heels and the sequins, or the masks and cloaks of superheroes.

### OUTFITS TO MAKE OR MODIFY

Small children find wrap-around cloaks and pull-on skirts with elastic waists easier to put on. If fastenings are needed, choose velcro. Outfits do not need to be elaborate or even complete. A modified hat, a cloak, or a fake-fur tunic is often all that is required.

### I'M A CAT

A perfectly acceptable cat can be made by adding ears to a black wool hat, a tail to a pair of black trousers, and making a tunic (see panel opposite) from black fake fur. Paint on whiskers with face paint or eyeliner.

### KNIGHTS OF OLD

Make a tunic (see panel opposite) from white felt. Cut out a cross from red felt and stick this to the chest. Complete the outfit by buying a plastic helmet and sword.

## JUST OLD CLOTHES

Rummage sales and thrift shops are the best source for mix-and-match dressing-up outfits. Children will like oversized shoes and coats; gold dancing slippers; feather boas; anything with sequins, satin, or fake fur. Mesh curtains make great ghosts and brides.

## ESSENTIAL PROPS

The best prop boxes have all or some of the following: handbags, wigs, witches' hats, fairy wings (stock up at Halloween), sunglasses, real glasses (with the lenses taken out), face paint, jewelry, old watches, hats, long gloves, wool hats with ears sewn onto them, mesh curtains, magic wands, and swords.

# How to make a tunic

Cut out an oblong of material (or paper) twice the length from the child's shoulders to the top of his legs and the width across his chest.

Fold the material in half, and cut out a hole for the child's head.

Hem the edges, or use pinking shears. Fasten each side of the tunic at waist level with a piece of velcro.

# Ghosts and monsters

CHECKLIST

| | |
|---|---|
| age 3–4+ | |
| indoor | ✓ |
| no. of children | no limit |
| time | 30 minutes or more |
| help required | ✓ |
| messy | making costumes and ghost picture |

**EQUIPMENT**
- mesh curtains and green dye
- dark paper and white paint
- scary stories
- flour, water, and red food coloring
- sheet
- balloon and wig
- tights and pillowcases
- cotton yarn, black dye, and rubber bands

## What the child learns
To come to terms with her fears.

One of the feelings all small children must learn to deal with as they grow up is fear. Many small children are afraid of something in particular: dogs, mice, spiders, or the pictures in a certain book, for example. Most of all, though, they are afraid of the unknown or unknowable: ghosts, witches, monsters.

## what to do
### GHOSTLY THINGS
The easiest ghost costume to make and wear is a mesh curtain. If you do not have an old one, look for a curtain in your local thrift shop. Drape it over her head and let her haunt the house.

Make a ghost picture. Fold a piece of dark paper in half. Put a blob of white paint into the crease, fold the paper over, and spread the paint by pushing away from the crease. If instead of the blob of paint she writes a spell, that will become all ghostly, too.

### SCARY STORIES
Cuddle up with older children (by the fire if possible) and tell ghost stories.

Read books about monsters and witches.

Traditional stories are usually very moral. Sometimes the underdog wins; sometimes a small creature does something foolish and comes to a sticky end.

Always remember to laugh, to be silly, and, most important of all, to have a reassuring cuddle at the end of the game.

## MONSTROUS THINGS

Monster costumes take a little more imagination than a simple ghost one. Halloween is a good time to look for some inspiration. Here are some ideas to get you started:

A mesh curtain dyed a lurid green with sections splattered with red would make a reasonable start (make some flour paste, add red food coloring, and paint it on the fabric in pools and dribbles).

A sheet dripping in fake blood.

A balloon with a wig to make an extra head.

Tights stuffed with pillowcases for extra arms and legs.

Cotton yarn dyed black and fixed to rubber bands for hairy feet.

# Water, water

**CHECKLIST**

age 2–4+

| | |
|---|---|
| indoor/outdoor | ✓ |
| no. of children | no limit |
| time | 30 minutes or more |
| help required | ✓ |
| messy | ✓ |

**EQUIPMENT**

- water
- selection of cups, pitchers, and bowls
- sponge
- wading pool
- toys such as plastic ducks, boats, and fish
- craft sticks and paint to make fish (optional)
- umbrella or hat and plastic bag for the shower
- watering can

## What the child learns

Adding an imaginary element to a game teaches her to look at even the most mundane activities, such as washing up, in a new light. She'll also learn something about the nature of water and conducting simple experiments.

Whether she's daydreaming at the sink, sinking cups in the bath, or racing Pooh sticks under a bridge, water captures a child's imagination. A two-year-old will probably be quite happy with a bowl of water at the sink, a sponge, and a cup or two, an older child may want to create a more complex world of little boats, ducks, and waterwheels.

## what to do

### AT THE SINK

Turn on the faucet so there is a small but steady stream of water and let the child fill cups and pitchers. She can then pour at will.

Alternatively, she can carry out the same tasks with a bowl full of water, but she must submerge the cups to fill them. She can also explore how some materials absorb water and others do not, how some float and some sink.

### IN THE BATH OR WADING POOL

There is something about being in the water that encourages the child to play imaginary games. Her ducks are swimming to the end of the wading pool because someone is coming with bread. The enemy is trying to sink her boats (here they come with a water cannon), or mommy fish is going off to get some food for her babies. Encourage such play by providing the child with the right tools: a flotilla of boats, a family of ducks, a dozen craft sticks with little fishy faces painted on them.

## IN THE SHOWER
A small umbrella or a wide-brimmed hat encased in a plastic bag make a delightful noise if the child wears them in the shower.

## WATERING THE PLANTS
Let the child talk to the plants as she waters them and ask them how much water they want today.

## OUT AND ABOUT
Race sticks in the stream or throw Pooh sticks into the river from one side of the bridge and watch them come out on the other side. Tell stories about the ducks she fed as she walks home. There is always room for her imagination.

# Just a few big boxes

**CHECKLIST**

| | |
|---|---|
| age 2+ | |
| indoor/outdoor | ✓ |
| no. of children | 1–3 |
| time | 30 minutes or more |
| help required | to start |
| no mess | ✓ |

**EQUIPMENT**

- cardboard boxes
- paint and paintbrushes to decorate (optional)

## What the child learns

This is a game two-year-olds can play together, helping them make those first steps toward friendship.

Children seem to go into a world of their own when they sit in a box. These suggestions are variations on the sitting in a box theme, and are great for a couple of small children to play when they are at that stage when neither of them can initiate a game for them to play together.

## what to do

### JUST A BOX

Small children love to sit in boxes. You can turn them into tractors with wheels and grills, but for the youngest children, all you really need is the box itself.

### AIRPLANE

To make a box airplane for more than one child, you need six similar-sized boxes, each one big enough for a small child to sit in. This is more boxes than most of us store, so you may need to wait until you've collected enough.

For the fuselage, arrange four of them in a line, the last three open-side-up, the first one open-side-down. Place the other two face down on either side of the second box to form the wings. The children can now hop on board and fly away. You can decorate the boxes if you like, but two- to three-year-olds will probably not care whether you do or not.

# Tents

Children love to squeeze themselves into small spaces and to be out of sight without being out of touch. Whether it's just a blanket over the dining table or a tent in the yard, the magic of a camp can keep a small child amused all day long.

## what to do

### QUICK TENT IDEAS
Throw a large sheet over the kitchen table.

Throw a sheet over the clothesline, and weigh down the edges with bricks.

Hang a curtain in front of the lower bunk bed.

Pull out the sofa and put some cushions on the floor between the back of the sofa and the wall.

Put a blanket between two dining chairs.

Clear out the bottom of a closet, but make sure the child can open the door from the inside.

Put up a little shed for him in the yard.

Buy a small tent and pitch it on the lawn.

### TENT ESSENTIALS
Cushions and pillows.

Blankets and, outside, groundcloth.

A telephone to keep in touch (see page 212), some invisible ink (see page 82) to write secret messages.

A password and a secret handshake for anyone who enters.

**CHECKLIST**

| | |
|---|---|
| age 3–6 | |
| indoor/outdoor | ✓ |
| no. of children | 1–2 |
| time | 1 hour to a day |
| help required | to start |
| no mess | ✓ |

**EQUIPMENT**
- tent, real or improvised (sheets, blankets, cushions, curtains, and something to support them)
- closets
- small garden shed
- picnic (see page 210)
- tin-can telephone (see page 212)
- paper, candle wax, and paint for invisible ink (see page 82)

## What the child learns
Tents give older children privacy. For the younger child, separating himself from the family helps him to think about the complex issues of how his thoughts and feelings are distinct from other people's, something children come to understand when they are approaching the age of four.

# Picnic

## CHECKLIST

age 3–4+

| | |
|---|---|
| indoor/outdoor | ✓ |
| no. of children | 2 or more |
| time | 1 hour or more |
| help required | to make the picnic |
| no mess | ✓ |

### EQUIPMENT

- picnic basket
- food and drink
- cloth
- cups, plates, etc.

## What the child learns

This is a special treat for two or more friends; it helps to cement friendships and fires their imaginations.

There is something rather special about a picnic, especially if your child has a friend, or friends, around to play. They do not need to go far: behind the sofa, under the table, in the yard. It's having it all packed in a basket and eating by themselves that fires their imagination.

## what to do

### THE PICNIC SPOT

On a cold or wet day the best place for a picnic is under the dining table or behind the sofa. Put a large cloth over the table to separate it from the rest of the room.

On a warm summer's day, the child can take her picnic into the yard. Let her choose her own spot.

## THE PICNIC

If they are going to eat outside, the children will need a picnic cloth big enough for them to sit on. Behind the sofa or under the table, a dish towel will suffice. They will also need a cup and a plate each.

They need something to drink. In the yard, let them pour their own drinks from the bottle into their cups. In the house, it's probably safer to give them a small bottle of water.

Make sandwiches, cut them small, and wrap them in foil. Include some cake and a piece of fruit for each child. Pack it all in a picnic basket. Let older children help you make the sandwiches and pack the picnic basket.

# Tin-can telephone

**CHECKLIST**

age 4–6

| | |
|---|---|
| indoor/outdoor | ✓ |
| no. of children | 2 |
| time | 30 minutes or more |
| help required | ✓ |
| no mess | ✓ |

**EQUIPMENT**

- 2 cocoa tins, snack containers, or paper cups
- wax-coated string
- skewer or knitting needle

## What the child learns

This is simple science or magic, depending on the child. It's a great social game.

Old-fashioned this game may be, but it is still fun: just magic for children to make and play. If the child has a tent, it's a great way to keep in contact with the base camp.

## what to do

You need two tins. These are going to be put against the child's ear, so they should not have sharp edges. Cocoa tins are ideal but snack containers and paper cups work, too. You also need a long length of string, preferably wax coated.

Make a hole in the bottom of each can with a skewer (for metal and paper) or with a hot metal knitting needle (for plastic). Parents

should do this for younger children and must supervise older children. Poke one end of the string through the hole in the can and tie it in a big knot inside the can. You may need to tie the knot a couple of times to be sure it does not slip through the hole when the string is pulled tight. Do the same with the other can and the other end of the string.

To play, one child whispers into her can and the other child puts his can to his ear to listen. This only works if the string is kept very tight—which will inevitably lead to the string being pulled out from the can, but it can easily be put back.

If you have a garden wall, try sending a whisper along it. One person whispers and the other puts his ear to the brick or stone. A slight curve in the wall helps.

# Construct

CHECKLIST

| | |
|---|---|
| age 4–6 | |
| indoor | ✓ |
| no. of children | no limit |
| time | 30 minutes or more |
| help required | to start |
| messy | ✓ |

**EQUIPMENT**

- packaging of all kinds
- adhesives: wood glue, adhesive tape, adhesive gum, double-sided tape, brass fasteners, paper clips
- string, yarn
- a special bag!

## What the child learns

To look at things and consider the possibilities. Lots of fine-finger skills, imagination, planning, and working toward an end.

Children love constructing things from boxes, oak tag, and bits of string. All they need is a collection of bits and pieces, some glue to fit them together, and a lot of imagination.

## what to do

### THE BUILDING MATERIAL

Collect packages: large and small boxes in various shapes, bits of oak tag, lids from screw-top jars and bottles, yarn, string, etc.

Prepare tubes. Empty paper towel and toilet paper tubes are very useful but a source of frustration. Whether placed on end or lying down, there is very little surface contact between a tube and a flat surface. To ease this problem, make four cuts at one or both ends of the tube and bend these back to make feet. Prepare some tubes with a single set of feet, others with feet at both ends.

Remember, most structures hold together better if they are built on a base of stiff cardboard. The sides of cartons are ideal for this.

## THE GLUE
Wood glue probably works better than paste.

Double-sided tape is excellent for tricky edges and corners.

Paper clips can hold things in place while the glue dries.

Brass fasteners allow wheels to move.

Tape reinforces glue, and holds things in place until they have dried.

## GETTING READY
The child may not know what he wants to make, so let him rummage through the box of materials and select what he is going to use before he starts.

Then move the box away and let him start with what he has chosen. If he finds he needs a special piece, let him look again. Having too much choice is distracting and leads to indecision.

Show the child how to apply the glue. Which bit must be glued is not obvious to small children.

# A useful bag

Buy or make a special bag in which to collect things for later games. Make sure the child has it with him when he goes out and about.

Help the child to look out for things to add to his nature table, or with which to adorn his constructions, collages, and mini-landscapes.

Keep the bag in the same (accessible) place so he can add day-to-day treasures to it.

# Roads and other layouts

**CHECKLIST**

| | |
|---|---|
| age 4–6 | |
| indoor | ✓ |
| no. of children | 1 |
| time | 30 minutes or more |
| help required | to start |
| not very messy | ✓ |

**EQUIPMENT**

- boxes, wrapping paper, self-adhesive sheets, or felt and bought and improvised toy furniture for the doll's house
- hardboard, papier mâché, sandpaper, mirror, paint, toy farm animals, and buildings for farms and towns
- oak tag, marker pen, adhesive tape, and toy traffic signs for roads

## What the child learns

To use his imagination. To play through his experiences, to remember, to learn about himself, and to develop his spatial skills.

Small children love playing with scaled-down models of reality. Doll's houses, garages, farms, and train sets are the classic examples of these little worlds. The preschool toy shops abound with such toys, but they are also quite simple to make. Here are a few ideas.

## what to do

### A DOLL'S HOUSE

Turn a box on its side. You can leave it as it is, or paper the walls with wrapping paper and put in a little piece of felt for a carpet, or use the self-adhesive material intended for lining drawers.

Buy or make some toy furniture. Matchboxes can be turned into beds or chests of drawers. Empty spools of thread with jar lids fixed on top make excellent tables; bottle caps make stools.

### FARMS AND TOWNS

A piece of hardboard makes a firm base for a farm or town. Add papier mâché hills (see page 156), sandpaper roads, and a little mirror for a pond. Paint the base green and add some plastic farm animals and little buildings from the toy shop.

### ROADS

To make a road system, cut lengths of oak tag, draw line markings, and fix the strips together with adhesive tape to form varying lengths of road. Add to the interest in the form of crossroads, turns, and intersections. Buy some traffic signs from the toy shop and then all the child needs is his model cars.

# Making little people

**Stick people**
These are wonderfully simple: Just draw faces on the ends of craft sticks. They work as they are or the child can add some straw or string hair or tie on an apron.

**Yogurt cup people**
Turn clean yogurt cups upside down and cover them with thin oak tag. The oak tag should be pretrimmed to size. Help younger children to fix it in place. An

older child should be able to manage, but if there is a problem, fix one end of the oak tag with double-sided tape. Stick the edges of the oak tag with tape.

Paint faces on the oak tag or use little gummed shapes to make eyes and noses. The child could use yarn or cotton for hair. Cut out little feet and attach them to the rim. They will need to have a small bit of leg attached to the foot. Attach the leg to the inside of the cup with adhesive gum or tape.

# Quick and easy puppets

**CHECKLIST**

| | |
|---|---|
| age 4–6 | |
| indoor | ✓ |
| no. of children | 1–4 |
| time | 30 minutes or more |
| help required | ✓ |
| messy | ✓ |

**EQUIPMENT**

- paper plates, oak tag, old socks or old sweaters, paper bags, and plastic bottles for the puppets
- bits of yarn, cotton, and felt
- rubber bands
- scissors
- needle and thread
- felt-tipped pens
- paint
- glue

## What the child learns

To use her imagination. To play through her experiences. To make things she can play with by herself.

Making things to order taps into many of the skills children need when they start school—following directions is, after all, what most early education is about. Here are some simple ideas for puppets. Making them is only the first part. The child can play with them when they are finished.

## what to do

### PLATE PUPPET

Attach two paper plates together (eating surfaces facing each other) leaving a space on one side big enough for the child's hand. Paint a face, glue or staple on yarn for hair, add a hat or a cork nose. The child just slips her hand between the plates and is ready to play.

### FINGER PUPPETS WITH A DIFFERENCE

Draw a body without any legs on some stiff oak tag. Make two holes near the base of the body so that the child can poke her fingers through to make the legs. She could make an elephant with one hole and poke a finger through for the trunk.

### SOCK OR SLEEVE PUPPET

A sock just needs a face; the sleeve of an old sweater needs a knot in the end and a face. If the child places her thumb opposite her fingers, she can use its big mouth to "speak."

### PLASTIC-BOTTLE PUPPET

Cut off the top of the bottle so you are left with a tube that can be decorated. Add a face and some hair or a hat or ears. The puppet sits on the child's hand and wrist and she bobs it up and down as the puppet speaks.

### PAPER-BAG PUPPET

Twist the corners of the bag to make ears, draw on a face, and you are ready.

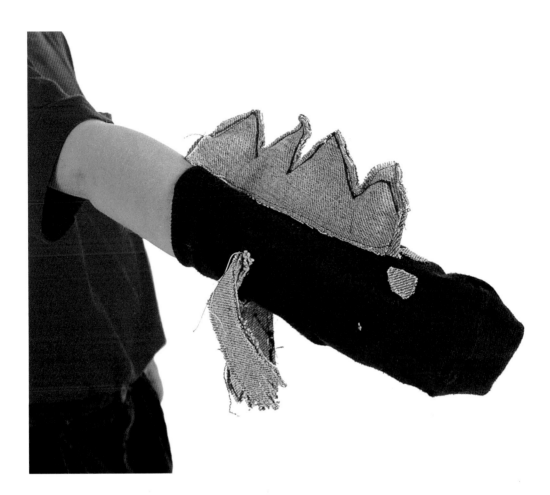

## GLOVE PUPPET

Stuff the toe of a sock with cotton, and keep the stuffing in place with a rubber band. It should be loose enough for the child to poke her finger inside. Cut off all but the last 3 in. (7 cm) of the sock. Decorate this head with a face and some hair.

Fold a piece of felt in half. Sew the sides of the felt together, leaving room near the top fold for a middle finger to poke out on one side and the thumb to poke out on the other. Make a small hole in the top fold and poke the sock head through this. Stitch this in place.

To play, poke the forefinger into the head and the middle finger and thumb out through the spaces at the side to make arms.

# Activity index

# General index

## Acknowledgments

| | |
|---|---|
| *Executive editor* | **Jane McIntosh** |
| *Project editor* | **Alice Tyler** |
| *Design manager* | **Tokiko Morishima** |
| *Designer* | **Ginny Zeal** |
| *Photographer* | **Peter Pugh-Cook** |
| *Stylist* | **Aruna Mathur** |
| *Senior production controller* | **Jo Sim** |

The publisher would like to thank all the children and
parents who participated in the photoshoot for their time,
energy, patience, and cooperation. Thanks also to the
following organization for allowing us to use their products:

**The Early Learning Centre**, South Marston Park,
Swindon, SN3 4TJ Tel: 01793 831300